ROUTLEDGE LIBRARY EDITIONS
BROADCASTING

Volume 2

A GUIDE TO COMMERCIAL RADIO JOURNALISM

A GUIDE TO COMMERCIAL RADIO JOURNALISM

LINDA GAGE

Revising editors:
LAWRIE DOUGLAS
AND
MARIE KINSEY

LONDON AND NEW YORK

First published in 1990 as A Guide to Independent Radio Journalism by Gerald Duckworth and Co. Ltd

Second edition published in 1999 by Focal Press

This edition first published in 2024
by Routledge
4 Park Square, Milton Park, Abingdon, Oxon OX14 4RN

and by Routledge
605 Third Avenue, New York, NY 10158

Routledge is an imprint of the Taylor & Francis Group, an informa business

© 1990, 1999 Larry Grant

All rights reserved. No part of this book may be reprinted or reproduced or utilised in any form or by any electronic, mechanical, or other means, now known or hereafter invented, including photocopying and recording, or in any information storage or retrieval system, without permission in writing from the publishers.

Trademark notice: Product or corporate names may be trademarks or registered trademarks, and are used only for identification and explanation without intent to infringe.

British Library Cataloguing in Publication Data
A catalogue record for this book is available from the British Library

ISBN: 978-1-032-59391-3 (Set)
ISBN: 978-1-032-64527-8 (Volume 2) (hbk)
ISBN: 978-1-032-64532-2 (Volume 2) (pbk)
ISBN: 978-1-032-64530-8 (Volume 2) (ebk)

DOI: 10.4324/9781032645308

Publisher's Note
The publisher has gone to great lengths to ensure the quality of this reprint but points out that some imperfections in the original copies may be apparent.

Disclaimer
The publisher has made every effort to trace copyright holders and would welcome correspondence from those they have been unable to trace.

A Guide to Commercial Radio Journalism

Linda Gage

Revising editors: Lawrie Douglas and Marie Kinsey

Focal Press

OXFORD AUCKLAND BOSTON JOHANNESBURG MELBOURNE NEW DELHI

Focal Press
An imprint of Butterworth-Heinemann
Linacre House, Jordan Hill, Oxford OX2 8DP
225 Wildwood Avenue, Woburn, MA 01801-2041
A division of Reed Educational and Professional Publishing Ltd

 A member of the Reed Elsevier plc group

First published as *A Guide to Independent Radio Journalism* by Gerald Duckworth and Co. Ltd 1990
Second edition 1999

© Larry Grant 1990, 1999

All rights reserved. No part of this publication may be reproduced in any material form (including photocopying or storing in any medium by electronic means and whether or not transiently or incidentally to some other use of this publication) without the written permission of the copyright holder except in accordance with the provisions of the Copyright, Designs and Patents Act 1988 or under the terms of a licence issued by the Copyright Licensing Agency Ltd, 90 Tottenham Court Road, London, England W1P 9HE. Applications for the copyright holder's written permission to reproduce any part of this publication should be addressed to the publishers

British Library Cataloguing in Publication Data
A catalogue record for this book is available from the British Library

Library of Congress Cataloguing in Publication Data
A catalogue record for this book is available from the Library of Congress

ISBN 0 240 51547 1

Typeset by Avocet Typeset, Brill, Aylesbury, Bucks
Printed and bound in Great Britain by Biddles Ltd, Guildford and King's Lynn

Contents

Foreword ix

Acknowledgements to the first edition xi

Acknowledgements to the second edition xii

Introduction xiii

1 **Equipment** 1
   Portable equipment 3
   Meters and levels 4
   Studio equipment 5
   News production booths 6
   Tape machines 7
   Leader tape 8

2 **Using the equipment** 9
   Recording 9
   Dubbing 11
   Editing 12
   Studio discipline 15
   Profanity 15

3 **Writing for radio** 17
   Remember the listener 18
   Telling the story 19
   Abbreviations 21
   Cues 22
   Your voice 24

4 **Finding the story** 27
   Basic sources 27
   News wires 28
   Independent Radio News 31

Internet 31
Reference books and sources 33
Archive sources 43

5 Telling the story 44
Reporting 44
Interviewing 50
Story presentation 55
News presentation 57

6 Programme production 60
The role of the producer 60
Programme preparation 62
Studio production 66
Programme formats 69

7 Responsibilities, objectivity and confidentiality 82
What is news? 82
Objectivity 83
Accuracy 85
Confidentiality 85
Good taste 87
Code of Fairness and Privacy 88
Other areas of responsibility 90
Complaints 92

8 The law and the courts 94
Introduction 94
Divisions of the law 95
Types of courts 95
Criminal courts 95
Civil courts 98
Judges' titles 99
Solicitors and barristers 100
Court procedure 101
Types of crime 102
Tribunals and inquiries 103
Coroner's courts 105
European courts 106
The Scottish system 107

9 Court reporting 110
General advice 110
Important sources 110
Reporting the criminal courts 112

10 Libel 116
What is libel? 117
Proof 119
Defences to libel 120
Damages 128
Criminal libel 129
Malicious falsehood 129
Scottish libel law 129

11 Contempt of court 131
Contempt of criminal courts 131
The Magistrates Courts Act 1980 132
The Contempt of Court Act 1981 134
Tape recordings of proceedings 135
During the course of a court case 136
Defences to contempt of court 137
Common law contempt 138
Scandalising the courts 139
Good faith 140
Interviewing jurors 140
The Scottish criminal justice system 140

12 Restrictions on reporting 141
Elections law 141
Formal orders restricting reporting 147
Rape and other sexual offences 148
Rehabilitation of Offenders Act 1974 149
Children and young persons 149
Preliminary and pre-trial hearings 150
Domestic proceedings and family law cases 151
New legislative restrictions, 1993–96 152
The Prevention of Terrorism (Temporary Provisions) Act 1989 152
The Official Secrets Act 1989 153
Freedom of Information Bill 153
Breach of copyright 154

Glossary 157

Further reading 168

Index 169

Foreword

by John Perkins
Managing Director, IRN

Radio – BBC and commercial – is a booming industry which attracts hundreds of aspiring journalists each year who want to get on the airwaves. Relatively few succeed and the difference between success and failure in most cases is an adequate understanding of exactly what the job entails.

Linda Gage's book is a valuable starting point for anyone who wants to make radio their career. It lays out in a practical and easy to understand way what it takes to make the grade as a good radio journalist – with the emphasis on the word 'good'. It is the sort of book I wish had been available when I started out in radio back in 1975 when you learned by your mistakes, which were often inflicted on the poor listener. Learning 'on the job' in this way may have been acceptable then but has no place in the sophisticated world of modern broadcasting.

Linda herself was a first class radio journalist who had the gift of passing on her knowledge of others. She was also an honest person, which is why this book pulls no punches and leaves the would-be radio journalist under no illusions as to what is required.

There are no signs of any slowdown in the number of new radio stations coming on air – just the opposite in fact – and there will therefore continue to be an increasing demand for journalists to produce the news and information which research consistently shows to be the most important ingredient in the radio mix. We should be grateful for this new edition of Linda's book, which will be required reading for many years to come.

Acknowledgements to the first edition

Watching other people get as smitten by radio as I am has always been a pleasure, but working at the National Broadcasting School gave me the opportunity to infect whole groups of people while in return teaching me a great deal. My gratitude goes to everyone there, especially Keith Belcher and Rory McCloud.

This book would not have been written without the encouragement, support and advice of many of my colleagues and friends. Everyone at what was LBC (now London Talkback Radio and LBC Crown FM) and at IRN has consistently made themselves available to me and my incessant questions, but those who endured more than their fair share of my fretting should at least receive a mention.

Lawrie Douglas first suggested I write this book, and he has never faltered in his faith in the project or in me – a specially important support during all those times when my own confidence waned.

Peter Thornton, the Managing Director of LBC/IRN, has always been positive and helpful, and Philip Bacon, the Editor of LBC Crown FM, gave up precious days to wade through the manuscript and make sensible suggestions. Roger Francis, the company's Chief Engineer, managed to explain to me complex technical concepts in words of one syllable, while the difficult job of trying to keep my sense of humour and of proportion usually fell on the shoulders of Robin Malcolm, the Director of Programmes for London Talkback Radio. Vivien Fowle and Sara Jones gave me valuable advice on particular chapters, and Deborah Blake at Duckworth poured an enormous amount of energy and time into it all.

A team of busy lawyers at Stephenson Harwood combed through my original notes on the legal chapters, while Larry Grant never lost his patience trying to correct some of my misconceptions about the law. It is also to his credit that I ate well during all those days of writing.

Acknowledgements to the second edition

Thanks are due to the following:

Tim Crook, CERT RAD JOURN, FRSA, an outstanding legal correspondent with LBC 1152, author and Head of Radio, Goldsmith's College, University of London. Tim has great depth of knowledge of the legal system and is responsible for updating and rewriting the legal sections of the book.
Colin Adams, Radio Clyde
John Greenwood
Sean Connors
Brian Hayes, of LBC and Radio Five Live
Darren Henley, Classic FM
Nicky Townley, LBC
Chris Mann, News Direct
Keith Belcher of LBC and Radio Liberty
Nigel Charters of LBC and now BBC
Hugh James, Cheltenham Radio
Justin Lockhart, Hallam FM and Magic 1458, Sheffield
John Perkins, IRN
John Pickford, Piccadilly 1152 and Key 103 Manchester
Rob Sims, IRN
Nik Walshe, Galaxy 105 Leeds
Malcolm Campbell, Charlie Rose and Mark Randall, Talk Radio
James Trend and Andy Ayres, Northern Media School, Sheffield Hallam University

Introduction

When commercial radio began in October 1973, very few people had experience of any system apart from the BBC. Most journalists came from newspapers or the BBC and had to learn new practices quickly. They were greatly helped by the large number of Australian and American journalists who came from countries where commercial radio had been in existence for half a century. Expectations and ambitions were high for the new (to Britain) idea of a twenty-four hour news and current affairs station, for local stations with quite large newsrooms that were keen to take on the BBC by introducing more local issues and voices.

Early hopes were dashed by many things – overambition, inadequate management, overoptimistic revenue forecasts, audience inertia, audience dislike of adverts, poor quality broadcasting. This forced many stations to rationalise their performance, opt for solvency and give listeners what they thought they wanted to hear. Within a few months of launching, the now giant Capital Radio, for example, shut down its large newsroom, sacked its journalists, decided to concentrate on music and made a lot of money.

Those stations that persevered with news and current affairs, however, have made a difference to the way they have been presented and developed :

- the pace and length of bulletins
- the range of voices and accents
- the development of the phone-in and of discussion programmes
- the use of the phone vote
- the first national phone-in at election time
- the more informal tone and approach towards authority, particularly in parliamentary coverage
- the demystifying of financial coverage, started by Douglas Moffitt in particular
- the twenty-four hour news and current affairs format
- the 20:20:20 minute format and concept of rolling news
- the inclusion of more entertainment and sports items in bulletins

Radio newsrooms have changed radically since the late 1980s when Linda Gage was writing her book. The job of the radio journalist, too, has changed. ITN's ownership of IRN and deals made with television companies mean that actuality of national and international leaders comes largely from television. Bimedia arrangements give ITN reporters the opportunity to provide radio versions of their television reports. Station reporters present, shape and package stories more. They have the technology to get good quality interviews without having to leave their desks. The story count rises but interviews at a distance lose the edge and tension of the face-to-face interview.

You will look hard to find a copytaster or an intake editor. Radio journalists report, record and edit their stories; they read bulletins; they load trails and ads. Editors, managing editors and programme controllers all read bulletins. The separation of jobs of the 1980s no longer exists.

There may be fewer reporters and there may be fewer news programmes, but there has been an increase in the number of journalists working in studios. They work as telephone operators; they drive the studio desks; they produce programmes and they present a wide range of news and current affairs programmes. Features and documentaries are thin in schedules and there are fewer recorded programmes. There is a much greater emphasis on live broadcasting which, despite its rawness and lack of polish, has immediacy. And there is always the danger that someone will say something unexpected and controversial that will later be regretted and might make the headlines. This move to live broadcasting has pushed the treatment of news and current affairs away from more formal reporting to being integrated into discussion and phone-in formats.

The number of journalists may have risen but starting salaries, at least, have fallen. Shift rates are about the same but contributors fees are, if anything, less than ten years ago. Whereas journalists on work experience were paid in the 1980s, this is no longer the case. And work experience and trainees at least had shadowing shifts to familiarise themselves with programme operation; again that has also disappeared. Much of training and education, itself, has moved away from the industry and into universities and colleges.

The sound of the news is different. It was always pacey but where once politics and the economy dominated the news, now you will find far more entertainment, showbusiness and sport items.

The network of independent local radio stations has burgeoned. Well over 200 stations exist. There are national and regional stations; there are local stations. Gaps in coverage are being filled in with district and borough stations. The distribution of IRN has moved from landlines to satellite and is likely to be sent by the internet next.

The quality of reception will improve with the introduction of Digital Audio Broadcasting (DAB). No more will we have to keep fiddling with the aerial when we move from room to room to get a good signal. But what will it mean for the journalist? Will it mean additional tasks? The DAB receiver will include not only a loudspeaker system but also a screen which will display text and graphics. And station owners will want to use DAB for the transmission of data.

Journalists may not have to develop new skills as such but will be asked to perform different duties. In addition to their traditional role as reporters, news and current affairs producers, bulletin writers and news readers, they will have to develop their computer and IT skills; they will assemble, collate and transmit data; they will be adept at using the internet as a resource; they will know how to programme remote stations.

Since the first edition was published there are more reporting restrictions and the scope of what we can report has been narrowed. Libel remains a shackle and major financial risk despite liberalising trends in Australia and America. We have become closer to Europe, and the European Convention of Human Rights is likely to become statute law in Britain with positive and negative implications for the journalist. The technology is faster so decisions and pressures are greater which accelerates the risks.

There will always be controversy about whether quality will suffer in the new climate and whether there will be enough advertising revenue available to support so many new stations. This will lead to the investigation into new forms of financing stations. Will sponsorship be allowed? Will more cross-media ownership come into being?

It's an interesting future.

CHAPTER 1

Equipment

The invasion of the computer has changed the face of radio news and the revolution isn't over yet. The days of clattering typewriters and wire service machines spewing miles of paper have long since vanished and the use of magnetic tape in news gathering and transmission is in swift decline. That's not to say the vision of a paperless, tapeless newsroom is a reality everywhere. Newer stations have signed up completely to the new technology and in some there isn't a tape machine to be found. Others have yet to embrace the changes. Most are somewhere in between (Figure 1.1). All that hasn't changed is the pace. Journalists still work with one eye on the screens, one

Figure 1.1 The newsroom at Hallam FM/Magic 1458 AM, Sheffield (photo: Marie Kinsey)

2 A Guide to Commercial Radio Journalism

ear on the monitor, and a phone clamped to the other ear. They just don't have to shout as loudly.

The new equipment has done nothing to minimise the almost traditional friction between journalists and engineers – who themselves are having to keep abreast of sometimes bewildering change. Engineers still complain that journalists don't know how to use the equipment, and that computer crashes are as much the result of operator error as software failure. But to do your job well you need the machinery. Learn as much as possible about it and treat it with the respect it deserves.

Computers first replaced the typewriter and newswire printers. Since the mid 1980s radio journalists have been calling up stories, reading newswires, writing scripts and sending messages to each other on several types of networked systems. As computers became more powerful, the IT industry developed ever more sophisticated software and hardware which added on audio editing facilities. The advent of digital telephone lines called ISDN circuits (Integrated Services Digital Network) means audio can be passed around stations via direct dial-up lines often connected by satellite. Many stations now take IRN material direct into their own computer system. It's this ability to move around both script and sound which has hastened the demise of traditional tape.

The move from tape based analogue technology to the new computer based digital systems means it's possible to achieve better and more consistent sound quality. When radio starts digital transmissions – and if digital receivers become popular (Figure 1.2) – there

Figure 1.2 A digital receiver

should be no deterioration in sound quality from the moment of recording to the moment your listeners hear it. That's because of the fundamental differences in the way both systems work.

Tape is a piece of plastic coated with tiny magnetic particles. When sound hits the tape electronically via the recording head of a machine it turns the head into a magnet of varying strengths according to the amount of sound passed over it. This agitates the magnetic particles on the tape and re-orders them, thus storing the sound. When the tape passes over the playback head the magnetic particles set up an magnetic field in the tiny gap between the two sides of the head. That makes an electric current flow which is then amplified to audible levels.

While the quality of tape has improved dramatically, and clever noise reduction systems have minimised the hiss which exists on all tape, the basic variability of the range of sound recorded means when a recording is copied onto tape elsewhere there's a deterioration in quality. Over time, the tape itself deteriorates, particularly if it's used over and over again – which often happens in newsrooms. Not so with digital recordings. The orginal sound is converted into a series of binary numbers based on zeros and ones, known as 'bits' of information. Since computers are designed to work with such numbers it's easy for them to store the signal and there's no degradation, because each bit of information can only ever be 0 or 1.

In practice you're likely to come across both old style tape based equipment and new style digital systems.

Portable equipment

There are four main types of portable recorders in common use: Marantz cassette recorders, Sony Pro Walkman, Sony DAT recorders and Sony Minidisc recorders. The first two are based on analogue technology, the latter two are digital machines. All are compatible with whatever studio equipment is used.

The Marantz is a professional American-made cassette machine which includes a feature that allows for some speed variation – a lifesaver if the batteries begin to die just as the interview gets good.

Cassettes come in various lengths, but most reporters are issued with C60s, which allow 30 minutes of recording on each side.

Cassette machines use tape which is only ⅛ of an inch wide and operate at a speed of just 1⅞ ips. Their disadvantage is that you cannot directly edit the tapes.

The choice of functions on cassette machines is pretty much the same regardless of type. Rewind and fast forward buttons are usually on their respective ends, embracing play and record, and sometimes pause and/or edit.

The size and weight of the Sony Pro speaks for itself, but Sonys are rarely company issue because they are not as robust as the Marantz.

DAT stands for Digital Audio Tape. Instead of using record and playback heads as the Marantz and Sony Pro do, a portable DAT recorder uses a slow speed tape scanned by a revolving head – exactly like a video cassette. The tapes are much smaller than a standard cassette but can still record an hour's sound or more. As the name suggests, the signal is recorded digitally – a big advantage if it's then to be edited on and broadcast via computer.

The Minidisc also records digitally on a compact disc about half the diameter of a conventional CD, although it does compress the sound slightly. It has all the CD advantages of being able to instantly locate tracks and scan through them, with easy identification on a display on the front of the machine. With a bit of experience, many reporters find they can do a rough edit in the field by marking up sections of the interview as individual tracks and erasing what they don't want.

The Sony Pro, Sony DAT and Sony Minidisc machines all have the advantage of their small size and good quality, although they're not as robust as the Marantz. There are particular problems with the microphone socket and line in/out socket, which take a mini jackplug. Not only is it easy to get the contacts dirty, they can break altogether. Short battery life is also a problem – the last thing you need just when the Prime Minister has given you that exclusive! To solve these problems, some stations have invested in conversion kits for DAT and minidisc recorders, which put the basic machine into a box equipped with longer life batteries and more robust XLR sockets.

But as the price of these new generation machines falls, some reporters decide to invest in them personally. If you do this, be careful in your choice of microphone. Since reporters deal mainly in the spoken word, a stereo mike is unnecessary, but be sure to choose one that is of broadcast standard. An AKG D230 or the slightly cheaper AudioTechnica, for example, would stand you in good stead.

Meters and levels

Regardless of whether your recorder is analogue or digital, it's still up to you to make a good quality recording. To help you do this, all equipment carries meters to tell you whether the sound level is within prescribed limits. If levels fluctuate too much, the listener will certainly get fed up with having to adjust the volume control. Levels also need to be controlled for technical reasons. If the level is too low for a sustained period of time, the transmitter will try to find some sound to boost artificially, while if levels go too high, the sound becomes distorted and difficult to understand. But equipment meters are really only there as a back-up because the most important meters are your ears. If the recording is 'compressed' so that the upper and lower ranges of sounds are forced into the middle range your ears will tell you to peak lower.

There are two systems of monitoring sound levels: VU (volume unit) and PPM (peak programme meter) and there are three ways of displaying this information: LED (light emitting diode), LCD (liquid crystal display) and a wagging needle.

The VU scale shows the average recording or playback levels rather than the peaks, and you tend to find them on cheaper equipment. The peak level is '0', and above that the meter literally goes into the red.

PPM measures the high peaks of sound, but does not fall back instantly, making them easier to use than VUs. Sound should normally peak at between 4 and 6 for speech, but check the particular station's policy.

LED displays consist of rows of lights which change colour from yellow to red. You should only get slightly into the red in the loudest parts.

LCD displays tend to be found on minidisc and DAT recorders. A row of blocks will shade in against a scale.

Studio equipment

As digital equipment, computer based word processing and editing software has transformed the face of the newsroom, so it's altered the make up of the main control room and smaller production booths. Most now have enough variety of equipment to cope with analogue and digital recordings (if the conversion is not yet complete!). Some simply have a series of computer screens holding ads, jingles, scripts, running orders and audio clips for news bulletins. There will also be CD players and a minidisc player or two. All of these are wired into a mixing desk.

In the control room computers have replaced two main pieces of equipment: large open reel tape machines and cartridge players. Cartridges, or 'carts', used to hold ads, jingles and trails, are simply a small pastic box containing a single loop of tape of varying lengths. When a cart is being recorded the machine puts an inaudible pulse at the start of the recording (the 'cue pulse'). The machine will automatically stop the cart at the pulse so that it is cued at the beginning of the recording and ready for air. Cart machines, however, do not have erase heads, so they must always be bulk-erased before you record onto them, and you must always play back your recordings to ensure you did not start with a 'dirty' cart.

Some stations still keep an open reel tape machine or two in control rooms and production booths and some have replaced the cartridge, or 'cart' with a digital version – Dcart – which stores the item on a floppy disc.

The mixing desk has more than one 'channel', or source of sound, and is either operated by an engineer or 'self-opped' by the presenter. Which channel is heard is decided by which faders are open. If there is more than one fader up, then sounds are being mixed together in some way. It could be as simple as two microphones being faded up for an interview, or it could be some combination of all the other equipment available, like music from a CD being mixed with a prerecorded sound-track off one of the computer screens, and a reporter talking over both.

Control rooms are laid out so that whoever is operating the desk can easily reach the equipment, with the ads, which will usually be on computer, arranged numerically.

Main control rooms are linked with a studio, and the two sides look at each other through a specially sound-proofed window. They speak to each other through a system known as 'talk-back' which allows the control room to speak to the presenter without being heard either on the piece that is being recorded or on air during live programmes. The presenter can also speak to the control room but, obviously, not when the microphone is on.

Studios are usually organised around some sort of round table with microphone leads fed through a hole in the centre. Presenters sit on the side of the table that commands the best view of the control room, while guests often have their backs to it. Apart from the obvious advantages of this arrangement, it is sometimes helpful for the guest to be unable to see the producer or engineer, who will often indicate visually that the interview is boring and should be wound up.

News production booths

Most independent local stations broadcast a combination of music and news bulletins, and their bulletins are usually broadcast from a separate, smaller production booth (Figure 1.3). These generally contain a computer screen and a mixing desk with a smaller capacity than the desk in the main control rooms. Some may have a cassette player/recorder, an open reel machine and a cart player, either analogue or digital. If booths have been designed to record only

Equipment 7

Figure 1.3 Newsreading at Picadilly 1152/Key 103, Manchester (photo: Marie Kinsey)

interviews (like most of the booths attached to news operations), they will not have any CD players or turntables. Booths are designed as 'self-op' areas, which means the journalist or DJ rather than an engineer controls the equipment. They are only large enough for one or two people.

Tape machines

If open reel tape machines are still to be found they are likely to be the workhorses of the newsroom: Studer A801 or Revox PR99BV (Figure 1.4). These professional machines have three 'heads' – the small metal rectangles that convert electric pulses onto or off tape. These are erase, record and playback. They appear in that order (reading left to right), because logic dictates that the tape is first erased, to allow the recording, which is then played back. If the machine is not in record mode, the first two heads are simply bypassed.

Video tape can be used to record sound only, and the quality is much better than recording tape. Most ILR stations use it as logging tape to retain the station's output for up to three months.

Figure 1.4 Revox reel-to-reel tape machine (photo: Marie Kinsey)

Leader tape

In order to show where the actual recording starts and ends, and to allow the tape to be 'lined up' on the studio tape recorder so that it is ready to start at just the right place and time, you splice on leader tape.

Leader tape should be spliced tight up against the start (or end) of the audio so it can be used as an accurate visual guide. Do not get carried away with leader tape. There needs to be enough of it to be able to get a firm bite when it is being lined up in the studio, but four feet is certainly sufficient. Miles of leader on the front of a tape can add crucial seconds to getting the tape ready for air if there happens to be a panic on. Similarly, use enough yellow leader so that bands can be spotted visually, but not so much that it takes longer to line up the band than it takes to read the link.

Twelve to eighteen inches of banding leader will usually be about right.

Bulk erasers

Bulk erasers are very strong electromagnets which destroy all the magnetic patterns made by recording on an entire tape. All old carts and reclaimed tape should be bulk-erased.

CHAPTER

2 Using the equipment

Recording

If you are in a self-op booth doing an interview, either with someone on the phone (a phone-out) or across the desk from you, you must keep an eye on the level and a hand on the fader in order to 'ride the levels' and keep them right (Figure 2.1).

If it is a phone-out, you will get much better quality if you dip the phone fader when you are asking a question, because the phone line will 'colour' your voice and make it sound odd. The phone fader does not need to go all the way down; how far you need to compensate

Figure 2.1 The newsbooth at Hallam FM, Sheffield (photo: Marie Kinsey)

will depend on the desk and the line, so use your ears. Obviously you must take your mike fader all the way out if you want to clear your throat or make any other noise.

If you are doing an interview down the telephone, it is a Radio Authority regulation that you must make it absolutely clear to the interviewee that you are recording the conversation for possible use on air!

If the interviewee is across the desk from you, learn how to keep a peripheral eye on the meter without losing eye contact with the guest. Some people will be put off if you seem obsessed with the equipment.

If guests kick the table while crossing their legs, or have a habit of tapping the desk to emphasise a point, great thumps will come through on the recording, and those points will need to be gone over again without the thumps. The most magnificent thumps are made by accidentally bumping the mike itself. Don't worry, your deafness is only temporary.

The reason you are deaf, of course, is because you are wearing headphones, which you must do whenever you are doing anything in any studio. The headphones, or 'cans', give you an accurate reflection of what is happening on the recording or on air; your ears can lie to you, or simply not hear as much as the microphone picks up. If you are involved in anything live on air, talk-back from the control room will go into the cans even when the mike is on, so it is the fastest way a producer or engineer can communicate with you.

When you are recording out in the field, whether or not you wear cans will depend on your equipment. Minidisc and DAT recorders do not have speakers so it's advisable to monitor the recording through the headphones as you make it – you'll have to check it back that way anyway. Cans or not, your ears must be sensitive to the atmosphere you are working in and to any extraneous sounds that could make editing the tape impossible, or become acutely annoying to the listener. If, for example, you are doing an interview and a plane flies overhead, you will not be able to edit the material recorded over the plane noise because it will be noticeable to the listener. And if an important point the listener should hear is being made during all this, forget it – the listener's concentration will be focussed on the plane.

The noise may actually make a point in itself if, for example, the interview is about the level of noise planes make. Excellent reports were filed when residents of a Cheshire village were complaining about the extra noise they'd suffer if a new runway was built at Manchester Airport – and the interviews just had to stop when planes were making their final landing approach. But keep your ears open for sounds you do not want, interrupt the interview, apologise to the interviewee, try to put him or her at ease again, and then ask the last question again.

If you are recording in a busy street, you will have to get the microphone as close to the interviewees as possible in order to have more of them than traffic noise. Watch your recording levels: you will have to bring them right down to compensate for being so close. Make similar allowances when recording in large rooms with high ceilings and bare floors. They tend to be natural echo-chambers and are jarring to the listener when the recording is dropped into a studio-quality programme. If there are curtains or anything else that will absorb some of the reverberations, do the interview in that part of the room, but still be conscious of working with the microphone closer to the interviewee than normal. That way you will make the mike concentrate on the voice, not the echo.

If you have a machine with an automatic level control (ALC), you are best advised not to use it. When ALC is switched on, the machine will automatically bring up any sound it can find to the peak level, including background noises while someone is taking a breath or considering a point. Apart from the fact that it sounds odd to the listener, this, too, can make editing difficult.

Whenever you are using a portable tape machine, be extra careful with the mike lead. The vulnerable bits are where it comes out of the machine and into the mike itself. Take special care if you're using minidisc or DAT recorders with minijack plugs. If the lead on either of those ends wobbles around you will get 'mike rattle' – clicks and thumps that obliterate the noise you wanted to record. Be sure that the lead coming out of the machine will not bump against anything, and then loop the lead at the other end around your hand so that the lead does not move back and forth as you move the microphone. Grip it firmly, but do not let the lead rub against the mike – that produces a squelch of its own.

Most important of all, remember that without your machinery you cannot do your job, so treat your recorder like any other piece of valuable property. Don't lose it, loan it, or leave it lying around!

Dubbing

Whether your interview is on minidisc, DAT or cassette, it will have to be dubbed before it can be edited and go to air. A dub, derived from 'double', is a copy of any source to any other. You will need a lead with the correct sort of plugs to fit into the line out channel of your machine and the input of the machine or desk you are dubbing to or through. While you are dubbing, watch your levels and keep your ears open to monitor quality.

12 A Guide to Commercial Radio Journalism

If you have an interview that is ridiculously longer than required, only dub off those sections that are going to make it into the final version.

Editing

It is only the very exceptional interview that goes to air without some edits. The purposes of editing are:

- To get rid of unwanted material. Whether it is to bring an eight-minute interview down to four, or cleaning up pauses or stammers.
- To rearrange the order. The answers to questions four and six may both be interesting and worthy of being left in, but if answer number six is more newsworthy, it should come before answer four.

But be careful that you never change the meaning of what is said, omit qualifications to statements or comments, or edit material to give the impression of a conversation going on, or answers being given, to questions put in other interviews.

Also take care not to confuse the listener by leaving in phrases like 'As I've just said ...' and check for time sensitivity. If an interview is recorded on embargo for bulletins the following morning, a bulletin editor will not be impressed if the audio clip contains the word 'tomorrow'. Similarly references to 'yesterday' hardly give the impression of an up to the minute news service.

You should aim to edit an interview so the listeners can't hear the joins. Try to match natural speech rhythms as far as you can, which can mean leaving in the thoughtful pause or an intake of breath. Taking out every single breath can make people sound like automatons.

With experience you'll start to conduct interviews in such a way that needs only minimum editing. But somehow, editing always seems to take longer when the deadline looms!

Digital editing

There's a whole range of software used in independent radio for editing. More complex, multichannel computer programs with many fancy effects – like Sadie, ProTools and Diaxys – tend to live in the commercial production studio while news systems are a lot simpler and usually come attached to the general news production system –

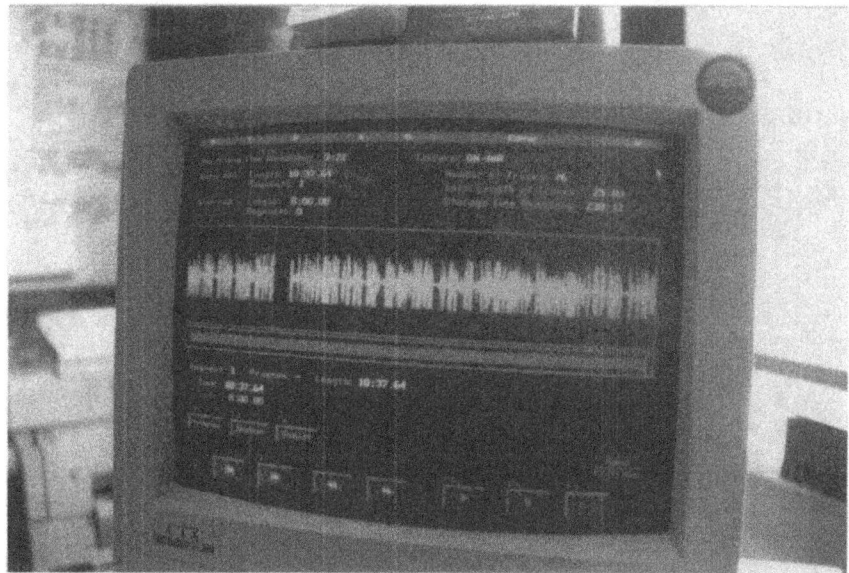

Figure 2.2 DAVE audio editing system (photo: Marie Kinsey)

in other words they're a mouse click or a touch button on your workstation screen. DAVE, CoolEditPro, RCS, Dalet and Audiovault are just a few. A big advantage, along with speed, is that editing on computer puts an end to crawling around the floor looking for that minute piece of tape you shouldn't have cut out after all. No matter how many edits you make, the original remains intact. So if you do make a mistake or change your mind, all is not lost.

All editing software programs work by displaying the recorded sound as a visible line known as a waveform which shows the peaks and troughs of the recording (Figure 2.2). You edit by using the mouse to drag a cursor across the screen to highlight sections you don't want then get rid of it by another click on the mouse. Some systems have a limited library of effects like mix and fade and will compensate levels if they're a bit too high or low. Some also give you an option of enlarging a section of the interview to help you place the cursor more precisely. You then name and save the file and store it in the relevant part of the system.

Some news editors complain that the ease of computer editing makes people careless: reporters don't try their best to get the best bits of the interview. Others say its far easier to be precise.

The biggest pitfall is the tendency to use your eyes and not your ears. Radio is about sound and just because there appears to be a gap in the waveform (Figure 2.3), it doesn't mean it should automatically be edited out. Listen first, then look should be the golden rule.

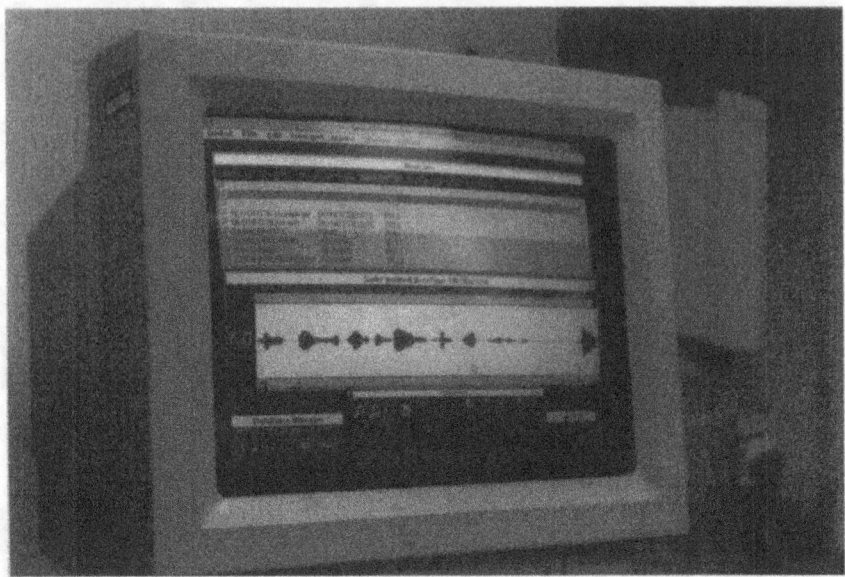

Figure 2.3 DALET computerised newsroom system, Hallam FM (photo: Marie Kinsey)

Tape editing

Editing tape is a different matter. Everybody is all thumbs to start with, and it is only through practice that it becomes a skill that can be performed well, even under intense pressure of time.

The main way of editing tape is known as the 'splice cut'. You need:

- an open reel tape machine with exposed heads
- splicing block
- chinagraph (grease) pencil
- single edged razor blade
- splicing tape

A splicing block has a groove down the middle which is fractionally less than the width of ¼ inch tape, and there are two or three slots across it at different angles. The block holds the tape securely so that a precision cut can be made.

A chinagraph, or grease pencil, is used to mark where a tape is to be cut. Since that mark is made while the tape is stretched across the playback head, a pen, ordinary pencil or the like should never be used. A well-sharpened chinagraph will make a precise mark without damaging the head.

Studio discipline

Studio discipline is important because it is not possible to create a good radio programme without all those involved in it hearing it. If the presenter does not hear the individual items, it is not possible to engage the skill of integrating them into a whole programme. If a producer is not listening to a live interview, there is no way of knowing whether all the pertinent points have been covered. And so on.

So the first rule of studio discipline is silence. Be sure that the things that need to be said are clearly understood, and then shut up. Never shout: it is inevitably a sign of panic.

If you do have information that needs to be imparted, be sensitive with your timing. Do not, whatever you do, distract the engineer when an 'out' cue is imminent or unnecessarily distract a presenter by using talk-back during a live interview.

Guests should only be allowed into a control room when the producer or the engineer agrees, and they must speak in voices low enough to allow the team to keep listening to the programme. Otherwise ask them to leave.

When it comes to decisions, the second rule of studio discipline is that it is the producer who makes them. The engineer may question the technical quality of an item, but the producer decides whether the story is big enough to warrant inflicting it on the listener. The presenter may suggest changes to the order in which items are to go out, but the producer decides.

The reasoning behind this rule is simple. If there is anarchy on a programme, that is what the listener will hear, so one person has got to make the final decisions, and those decisions must be made clear to everyone concerned and accepted even if they are wrong.

Profanity

'Profanity', or prof, is the term generally used for a delayed broadcast. British Telecom requires any station that runs phone-ins to have a delay system 'available', but it does not insist that it is used. The Radio Authority recommends that all phone-ins or programmes that let members of the public on air should be 'in profanity'.

The way prof works is as follows. The output of the live programme is sent from the studio to a piece of equipment called a digital delay unit. This prevents the programme from being fed to the transmitter for up to ten seconds, so that if anyone swears, libels someone, commits contempt, or whatever, the producer or presenter in the live studio can press the prof button, and a jingle will be played to air instead of the offending remark.

The delay gap must be filled at the beginning of the programme while the machinery delays the broadcast. That gap used to be filled by inserting either the same jingle that will override any offensive remark, or a special one. Nowadays, the programme is usually put into delay during a news bulletin and the sound going to the transmitter is slowed down very slightly until the required gap exists between what is being said in the studio and what the listener hears. This does have the unfortunate effect of making whoever's presenting at the time sound slightly odd for the two or three minutes it takes to achieve the delay.

To come out of delay the procedure is reversed, and it's all done at the touch of an icon on the computer screen.

CHAPTER

3 Writing for radio

Before you sit down to write a script, consider the components of writing. Words are our stock in trade. We can use sound effects to bring the listener with us part of the way, but in the end it is our words that have to be precise and meaningful. Excellent books have been written on the use of English, but as a general principle, remember Sir Ernest Gowers's advice in *Complete Plain Words*: 'Think for others rather than yourself.' Assess your script before it hits the listener.

Think carefully about the words you choose to use. Words have precise meanings, and if you do decide to misuse them, you should at least be aware of what you are doing. For example, a word that is now commonly misused, especially by politicians, is 'refute' in place of 'deny'. The correct meaning of 'refute' is 'disprove'.

The other demon of the language is the cliché. Despite Sam Goldwyn's advice to 'avoid clichés like the plague', there may be an argument for using a cliché when that is the word the listener will understand without having to think about it. Which words are clichés, or at least over-worked, changes with time, but as a simple exercise, go through the papers, pick out the clichés and decide which word you would have used instead. The tabloids will give you a long list, but the 'qualities' will also provide a fair share.

When we are writing scripts, we try to find different ways to describe what has happened so that we do not sound repetitious, but do be careful not to use words of the wrong weight and tone. If something is 'claimed', is it said, declared, asserted, submitted, contended or maintained? Any one could be correct, but each implies slightly different motives.

Also, think about the construction of words. 'The ship was evacuated' is a fact, but 'The ship had to be evacuated' is a judgement that should be attributed.

Remember the listener

When writing for radio, you should aim to create vivid 'sound pictures' in the listener's mind. The listener has no way of knowing that your face is registering surprise or scepticism, or that you are looking out over a field that should be green but is parched with drought. It is your words that tell the story, so choose them on the basis of their weight, clarity and expressiveness.

Unlike a reader, the listener cannot stop and go back over what has been broadcast. You must therefore use words that are easily understood on first hearing.

You will find your job easier if you remember certain tried and tested guidelines, summarised as follows.

Logical

Your association of ideas should unfold in a logical way, so that the listener doesn't get lost along the way. Signpost changes of direction, e.g. by saying 'So in practice, it may happen like this.'

Idiomatic

Your language should be conversational in tone and style. Write as you speak, rather than according to the strict rules of grammar and punctuation. You can end sentences with prepositions, and add full stops to incomplete sentences if the result is a natural, conversational style. Use contractions: say 'don't' instead of 'do not' and 'can't' instead of 'cannot', etc.

Singular

You are talking to one listener. Don't talk about your 'listeners' or 'audience'. Talk to the single solitary listener as you would to a friend – don't talk down to or at that friend, but get the point across.

Terse

Limit your information. Don't overload your script with too much information. Your listener won't be able to take it all in, will lose interest and switch off (either physically or mentally). Try to cut through factual details and go for the whole picture. Avoid statistics, and if you must use numbers, deal in round numbers.

Easy

Your script should be easy to understand and follow. Write in simple, straightforward sentences. As a rule, try to stick to one idea per sentence. Use words that anybody will instantly understand.

Noteworthy

Be concrete. Talk in pictures and images to illustrate points. Avoid abstractions.

Expanding

The listener may not be able to absorb an idea right away, so expand on it until it is fully understood before moving on. When you need to repeat a point, find a new way of saying it.

Riveting

Your script should catch and hold the listener's attention. Try to involve the listener as much as possible by consciously seeking a response and provoking thought. Build word pictures and illustrate points with analogies. Vary your approach and use different angles.

Telling the story

This section has been written in radio style, so you should be able to read it out loud and make it conversational.

> Tell 'em you're going to tell 'em.
> Tell 'em.
> Tell 'em you told 'em.

Childlike simplicity is the essence of writing for radio. When people exchange news in the pub or over a cup of tea, they tell it in perfect radio style:

> 'Fred's been taken to hospital ...'
> 'Doreen's husband's left her ...'
> 'That Jones boy is in trouble again ...'

So tell the story as though you're telling it in the pub. Remember that your friends are educated and intelligent, but they may only half hear what you say at the beginning. If you say 'The Council Tax in Liverpool is to go up again', you'll grab their attention. But if you say 'The Finance Committee of Liverpool City Council reported last night that expenditure forecasts show an increase which may have to be passed on to householders', nobody will know what you're talking about ... and you'll run out of breath before the end of the sentence.

Treat the first sentence as your headline. It must grab the listener's attention and signal that you're saying something interesting.

Even after you've made the first bold statement, remember that the listener may only be half aware of what you said. How often do you have to listen again (where did he say that train crashed?) only to find the newsreader doesn't tell you?

So when you 'tell 'em', your second paragraph should repeat the main point, albeit in disguise:

'The average increase is expected to put fifteen per cent on council tax.'

So in telling the story, you first alert the listener, then inform: 'There's a major fire in Portsmouth Dockyard. A hundred homes in the Pitt Street area have been evacuated, but firemen say there's little danger of an explosion.'

Get to know as much about every story as you can. You can't write a good script if you don't know the subject, and the listener will always know when you're hedging. But even if you know all the details, don't get too involved in the minutiae of the story. Keep it simple and easy for the listener to follow. If you find it difficult to understand, the listener will find it impossible.

Don't overwhelm the listener with unnecessary complexities: 9.65 per cent is 'nearly ten per cent'; 900 yards is 'just over half a mile'; £4,898,247 is 'nearly five million pounds'.

If someone's being quoted in ordinary conversation, people usually start with their title or occupation. This gives an idea of how much importance should be attached to the statement, and also sounds more natural: 'The butcher says the price of lamb's going up,' not 'The price of lamb's going up next week, the butcher says.'

Start with the person's title or position. Don't start with a name unless the person is so well known that the listener will know who it is without having to think about it – Tony Blair, for example, or Elton John.

Use the present tense as much as you can. Newspapers have to print yesterday's news. The great advantage of radio is its immediacy, so emphasise it. If you're writing a story about something that happened in the morning for a programme that'll go out in the afternoon, don't use the past tense. Even if this isn't the first opportunity you've had to tell the tale, tell it in the present.

Avoid subordinate clauses. Marshal your facts in short sentences, avoiding commas or brackets:

> 'The horse, owned and trained by Mrs Mollie Clark and bought last year for fifteen hundred pounds from the Irish trainer, Jim Jones, former owner of the Derby winner Argos, is dead.'

Who's dead? While the listener is trying to work out who's died, he or she might as well be wearing ear-plugs. Anything else you say simply won't be heard.

Be sure you clearly understand the information that needs to be told. If French lorry drivers are blockading ports in France as part of a major strike, why are you telling me? Is it because people will find it difficult to drive to their second homes in the Dordogne or because jobs are at risk? If so, tell me in the first sentence. In France, the top line would be the strike itself. But we want to know how it affects us.

If you're writing about a foreign country, tell the listener where it is. Geography isn't everyone's strongest subject.

If you find that you're writing yourself into a corner, or that your copy's getting complicated, stop and ask yourself 'What's the point?' Remind yourself why the story is important and which points need to be made. Then get a clean sheet of paper and start again. It's worth doing this even if the deadline is pressing (and in radio, deadlines always seem to be pressing). Otherwise, the copy you send to air will be confusing and a waste of time.

While it's right to use contractions such as 'can't', revert to the full form if you want special emphasis: 'You cannot be serious!'

Although you're trying to squeeze as much information as you can into as few words as possible, it's sometimes better on the ear to use a longer form. It's headline journalese to say 'bid' instead of 'attempt', or 'probe' rather than 'investigate' or 'look into'. A 'shares price plunge after conciliation bid fails to win strike pact' may be understandable when you can read it twice, but that's a luxury radio doesn't offer. In any case, have you ever heard anyone in the pub talking that way?

Abbreviations

Very few initials should be used. Those generally recognised by the public are AA, RAC, TUC, NHS, RAF, BBC, IRA and RSPCA.

When you do use initials, identify them and clarify what they mean. For example, CBI = the employers' association; RMT = rail and seamens' union. When you can, leave the initials out: 'Teachers' union leader, Nigel de Gruchy'.

If you do use initials, give the full form first: 'Doctors at the British Medical Association want tougher warnings on cigarette packets. The BMA say the present regulations ...' not 'The BMA say there should be tougher warnings ...'.

Cues

There are very few ad libs on radio. Almost every word spoken is scripted in advance. Many presenters even script up the openings: 'Hello, welcome to the programme. I'm Joe Bloggs and today we're going to ...' It isn't that Joe Bloggs is afraid that he will forget his own name (though I have heard presenters read out their initials instead of their names because that was how it was scripted), it has to do with considerations of flow and timing.

Radio is governed by the clock, and you have to know how long everything will take. There are times when the introduction, or 'cue', to an item is longer than the actuality itself. While some flexibility can be built in, if you are planning to run a dozen stories in an hour-long programme, you have to know whether those items will leave the hour light, or whether you should re-edit some of them, or find earlier 'pots', in order to fit everything in.

A 'pot' is not a jam-jar. It is a place in the item where transmission can be stopped, even though it has not run its full length. Pots probably got their name from the old days of radio when volume was controlled by potentiometers, or 'pots', and an item could be ended early by turning the knob quickly to zero during a breath or pause. For practical purposes, though, it could stand for 'pulled off transmission'.

Finding pots on items before they go on air gives you flexibility, and means that you can get out of an item neatly if you are short of time or an important story breaks. Taking 'blind' pots, i.e. trying to second guess where to pot while the item is going out on air, is usually messy and could be dangerous for legal or contextual reasons.

There are various reasons why some items should not be potted, such as that the best bit is at the very end, or in the interests of balance. In such cases a note that the item is not pottable should go onto the cue.

The cue must fulfil the following functions:

- Grab the listeners' attention
- Summarise the story and directly introduce the recording
- Put the recording into context

A good cue will also act as 'insurance', giving the listener sufficient information to understand the story should the audio fail to materialise for some reason. But it should not give away the punch line.

The cue also carries operating information vital to the presenter, engineer and producer:

- The catchline, or 'slug', which identifies the story
- The date and time of writing
- The author's name, and an indication of other sources used
- The duration of the audio
- The first few words of the item ('In')
- The last few words of the item ('Out')
- The duration and outcues of pots
- The total duration of cue and audio combined

Some computers which have been specially programmed for use in broadcasting can calculate the total running time of both script and audio, but if you need to work out the duration of a cue manually, count three words as 1 second. In the case of a news cut, the cue gives the story number and the cut number.

A typical cue embracing all these programme requirements might look like this:

Indonesia /Hillman 1730 update Reuters/ 14 May

Rioting intensified in the Indonesia capital, Jakarta, this afternoon.
Supermarkets and shops were looted and set on fire. Foreign shop owners were often the target of attacks and several Chinese, including women and children, were killed.
The Indonesian president, General Suharto, broke off his visit to Egypt and returned home to deal with the situation.

Geoffrey Hillman reports.

IRN No.
DUR: 2:53
IN Q: RIOTERS BEGAN LOOTING ...
OUT Q: ... UNTIL THE MORNING.
TOTAL: 3:14
POT Q: ... AT ABOUT MIDNIGHT.
POT DUR: 1:32

This cue tells us that the story is about Indonesia, and that it is written by Geoffrey Hillman at 5.30 pm. It is updated, which means it supersedes any other tapes on Indonesia, and material from the

Reuters wire service was used in it. The date should be the date the item is to be transmitted: if you do not include it, an archivist somewhere will curse you. The item runs for 2 minutes 53 seconds, and the cue and item together will take 3 minutes 14 seconds, unless it is potted at 1 minute 32 seconds.

Never finish a cue with the same words as appear at the beginning of the item – it jars and sounds silly. For example, do not finish your cue with 'He told me he was exhausted' when the item begins 'I'm exhausted'. Find another formulation, such as 'He told me the experience was a test of his endurance.'

Your voice

You will have to find your own pace and style in front of the mike. Experiment with your voice – you will be surprised what you can do by varying your intonation and speed of delivery. There is no substitute for practice, but a few hints may speed the process up.

First of all, you are not talking into a microphone. You are talking to a friend who is sitting no more than six feet from you. Do not shout. Learn to convey urgency and authority by varying your pace and tone.

The listener should never be aware that you are reading from a script. 'Reading conversationally' (and without rattling the paper) comes naturally to some people, but most of us have to practise to get it right. Picturing your friend helps, because the apparatus and the thought that strangers are listening can be off-putting. So forget the mike, and just tell the story.

You must understand what you're reading. If you do not, you will not be able to give the story the correct stress and inflection. For example, read out the phrase 'What's the matter with you?' putting the emphasis on different words each time. The different stresses alter the meaning. Most presenters and reporters mark their scripts, underlining key words that need to be stressed and putting in back slashes or asterisks to show where they should take a breath or pause.

Quotation marks should not often appear in radio scripts. But when they do, you indicate their presence by a small pause both times and a very slight change of tone: 'Mr Prescott says the measures are // "too restrictive" // and thinks they should be withdrawn.'

Your delivery should be measured, no matter how fast or slow you go. The average speaking pace is three words per second. Some people naturally speak faster or slower than this, and you will have to see what your 'norm' is.

You should aim to speak fast enough to maintain interest, but slow enough to keep the listener with you.

Your voice must convey credibility. Be sure to project well; do not mumble, but equally do not bombard the poor listener or get so close to the mike that you pop. 'Popping' is an exploding noise that happens when a 'p' or 'b' gets thrown at the microphone so hard that it cannot cope.

Going back to the pub for a minute, as we sit and talk we communicate thoughts, and we think (and listen) in groups of words and phrases. Learn to read your script in the same way. This will depend somewhat on having a well-written script in the first place. If it's written conversationally, it can be read conversationally.

Your voice will also convey your facial expression. Just try to sound serious while reading with a smile on your face.

Read scripts aloud before you record them or go to air, so you know when a sentence or phrase is more than one breath's worth. Mark where you are going to take the extra breath.

Figures should always be written out. It is difficult to interpret a series of noughts on air, and if there is a typographical error in a written word, it will be less disastrous than if a figure is wrong. So write 'more than a million' rather than 'more than 1,000,000' and 'a hundred and thirty have died', not '130 have died'. If the script actually reads 'a hundred and thirty have died', the chances are that it will come out right on air, but if it reads '140 have died', there's no hope. And, although this is not the main consideration, writing figures out also keeps your word count accurate.

Just one additional word of caution about figures. In sports stories, does '0' mean nought, love, zero, oh, or nil? The listener knows, so if you don't, find out. A presenter at City in Liverpool once managed to light up the station switchboard when she reported that Liverpool football club had beaten a German team by 'four goals to love'.

You can speak loudly without shouting if you use projection. This is a skill that actors and singers learn, and so should you. Project your voice from your diaphragm, not from your vocal chords. To find out where your diaphragm is, you should first of all be sure you're in a room on your own so people won't think you've gone a bit peculiar, then pant like a dog. Keep panting for a couple of minutes (but be careful not to hyperventilate), and that horizontal band near your waist that begins to ache is it. Your diaphragm is a muscle, and like all muscles it gets stronger with use and exercise.

You can add authority to your delivery by lowering the register of your voice, which is especially useful for some female voices. Articulate the words of the script clearly, and pounce on them rather than allowing the words to trickle out. Remember that the end of the sentence is as important as the beginning, so do not let your voice trail off.

The most important thing is to know what you are talking about. It is credibility you are after, and that comes with knowledge, understanding and authority.

CHAPTER

4 Finding the story

Commercial radio's approach to stories tends to be punchier than the BBC's, and more colloquial language is used. Our delivery is different, our pace is usually faster, and over the years this has had an effect on the approach of the BBC.

There are times when even the choice of story will be different. Generally, the BBC tends to carry more foreign stories, while we concentrate more on domestic stories.

For all the differences between the services, if you put the editors together in a room their overall approach would not be very different. There is fierce competition to get a story to air first. If a big story breaks, everyone goes for the best, fastest and most thorough coverage. Since commercial radio is smaller and leaner, we do not have so many tiers to get through. This sometimes means we can scramble faster.

Basic sources

The most important source of news is your involvement in the community, knowing what is affecting it and what people care about. That involvement is vital if your news judgement is to be sound, but it is also your most basic source of information, whether national or local.

Journalists build up individual contacts over the years who become valuable sources of news. These are people who come to know and trust a particular journalist and will ring when something of interest or importance is happening. But individual contacts are the thoroughbreds in the stable. The workhorses form part of the day-to-day organisation of the newsroom itself.

The first general guide you turn to on any particular day is the 'news diary' – a compilation of all the news releases received by the station concerning events for that day. The hard news releases are separated from the 'what's on' variety, the former being of interest to the news desk, the latter possibly for use on air as a public service. Given that all newsrooms are flooded with news releases (stations in large cities can get hundreds in one day), you might think that they would generate a large number of stories. Alas, we do our duty and sift through them all, but well over 90 per cent of them meet their Waterloo with little more than a glance.

The diary will also contain reminders of events, anniversaries or updates for running stories, such as the starting date for an inquiry, the resumption of a court case, or the day a group of charity walkers are expected to return.

Apart from through the post, press releases flood in via fax machines and E-mails. Faxes should really be used only for urgent information that stands some chance of staying out of the wastepaper bin. In any case, fax copies are usually more difficult to read than the original. E-mail has the advantage of being very easy to read, to copy to computer files for general access and to re-write and edit.

The Press Association publishes a daily general prospects list, showing the major stories they will be covering on that day. It sometimes runs on the wire for the first time at about 04.30 and is then repeated later, or it may come across just once at about 08.30.

IRN also compiles a prospects list each morning in order to let all the stations in the network know which stories the editor intends to cover. An updated prospects list goes out during the day, updating stories and giving evening and overnight stories that will be covered.

Once those basic sources have been checked, it is a matter of check calls, tip-offs and keeping an eye on the wires.

News wires

News wires are information services hired out to clients. IRN and network stations have a variety of news wires available, the most widely used being the Press Association and Reuters.

Televisions in the newsrooms enable you to keep a check on Ceefax and Teletext, but their coverage tends to be brief – more like a headline than a full story – and the length of time it takes them to process stories often means we have already had the story to air before it appears on the screen.

The wires are used constantly, but for different things depending on the story and which job is being done. They may sometimes be used as a basis for voicing up a story before a reporter can get to the scene or before we can get actuality, but we also rely on our own sources, not only because it is good journalistic practice, but also because we need to be completely on top of stories immediately. The wires are designed for newspapers, so they may be slower than we can accept, and they are geared to deadlines that are anathema to us.

New stories can appear on screens at a rate of about fifty in ten minutes, so the wires are obviously feeding us a lot of information which needs to be sifted. Members of the newsdesk keep a check on everything running on all the wires and alert the editor to a new story or angle if necessary. In programme terms, producers and reporters scan the wires and use the information according to their needs.

Press Association (PA)

The Press Association has a staff of about 250 journalists and deals with domestic stories in the main, covering foreign stories only when they have a domestic connection.

Once a story has opened on PA, it continues to use the same slug for each subsequent up-date or rewrite.

PA gives you the story in short spurts or 'takes', and each take is numbered. In the case of the death of Diana, Princess of Wales, the number of takes went into double figures for several days. Each day's coverage starts with take number 1, and there are times when the takes do not even appear in chronological order. PA is used in the newsroom as a back-up service for details of stories or background. It is also a source for breaking stories, but we often get notice of a story from our own sources before it appears on PA.

Sometimes PA runs a 'snap' – a very brief indication that something important has happened, which is often not even in complete sentence form. In due course, it will put out a 'snapful' (a fuller write-through of the story), but this may take some time, which is another reason why we rely on our own sources.

Takes, snaps and snapfuls have been mentioned. Other terms you will come across include:

- Lead: a new write-through that may include new information.
- Substitute: a re-write of a story after a correction or after new information.
- Background: information which complements a running story. It does not necessarily give any details about the actual story that prompted the backgrounder.
- List: the day's diary of main stories and how PA will cover them.
- Advisory: a message telling you what to expect from PA and when, if it differs from the list.
- Diaries – both city and news.

The Press Association also provides sports, features and a city wire service.

Reuters

Reuters became a public company in 1984, and London is just one of its main bases, albeit the original one. Its computer slug is rtu. Reuters is an international news service, but we use it mainly as a source of foreign and financial news.

Like PA, Reuters gives you the story in spurts, but its takes are usually a bit longer. It employs about 1200 journalists in 80 countries and 181 cities, and that number is topped up by the use of 'stringers', or freelancers. Their terminology includes:

- Scheduled: an expected story which they had advised they would be covering.
- 1stld: 'first lead', a re-write which may include new information.
- Urgent: a major story that is just breaking.

Two-Ten Communications

This is a service which newsmakers can use. Clients (often companies or unions) pay to put out full statements or press releases on their wire. A Two-Ten journalist can write the story for them in journalese, or clients can hire its audio service to send a recorded Q & A to radio stations on DAT, minidisc or tape. Two-Ten also provides a studio for down-the-line interviews. The service is not used extensively by either newsdesks or programmes (except the city desk) because the subject matter is either too particular for us or, if they are running statements on stories we are covering, those statements will have come through directly to the newsroom.

Other wires

Some stations have a file containing several other news agencies, such as Associated Press.

Independent Media Distribution

IMD provides a syndicated item service concentrating on finance and entertainment from which several stations use the 'money minute'.

Metro and Bloomberg

Provide news, sport and finance coverage to radio subscribers.

Other sources

Newsrooms can monitor other radio stations and the many news programmes on terrestrial, satellite and cable television and the internet.

Independent Radio News (IRN)

IRN has access to all ITN material, which is especially helpful for major national and international news. There is also a bimedia arrangement whereby ITN reporters can provide a radio version of their stories. Arrangements to take in actuality are also made with other organisations, such as CNN and Reuters. But almost all staff are based in the London newsroom. The journalists who cover Parliament are based in the Millbank parliamentary complex.

IRN provides more than 200 network stations with national and international news. Stations can opt into the on-hour news live from the London studios, or compile bulletins locally from all the components that are regularly fed to them on circuits (including cues, cuts and snaps). IRN also supplies the network with headlines for half-hourly news summaries (Figure 4.1), and each hour a 'billboard' service of longer items.

The reader/writer reads each bulletin from IRN's London studio and is also responsible for writing and sending to the network summaries of the three or four main stories which will be read out at approximately half-past each hour. These headlines are usually no longer than one or two sentences, but must give the latest and most important angles of each story. The reader/writer will also help to prepare items for the bulletins that go out on the hour.

The duty editor decides which stories will go into each bulletin, and in what order, prepares the items and makes sure that the newsreader gets the right amount of material to fill the bulletin. Bulletins range from two to four minutes.

IRN reporters work in a staggered shift system, so that there are reporters available twenty-four hours a day.

Internet

This is an increasingly important and almost infinite source of information. The Internet stores information on a series of linked computers around the world. It does, however, require selective handling

Independent Radio News

**Monday 31 August 1998
The headlines at 22:03**

The US stock market's crashed as Russia's economic and political crisis continues to reverberate acround the world.

New York's Dow Jones index has ended today almost five hundred points down - that's it's worst day for twenty-five years.

Bill Clinton's on his way to Moscow for a summit with Boris Yeltsin whose presidency has suffered another blow.

The Russian parliament has overwhelmingly rejected Mr Yeltsin's choice for Prime Minister.

The Spencer family have held a memorial service at Princess Diana's island graveside on the anniversary of her death.

Forty people were at the lake on the Althorp estate to sing three hymns and hear a sermon from the vicar who carried out Diana's burial.

Three members of a British family have died in Florida after their mini bus hit a pick up truck as they drove to the airport to fly home.

Six other relatives were injured in the crash in Orlando.

Louise Woodward is asking British TV bosses not to follow America's lead and start televising trials.

The former au pair's told the Edinburgh Television

http://www.irn.co.uk/news.html   31/08/98

Figure 4.1 IRN headlines for half hour news summaries

and patience to achieve results. All entries must be checked and confirmed according to standard journalistic practice.

It includes a host of directories, called Search Engines, which organise the information into categories and hierarchies and make it more easily accessible for people. Search Engines run programmes with names like crawler, spider or worm, which store the information in an online database. And most of them have News pages on their websites, which are continually updated. Good examples are Yahoo! UK and Ireland (Figure 4.2) and WebCrawler (Figure 4.3) . All Search Engines have categories to select from, e.g., Arts, Politics, News, Science, Sport. Although most are basically American, they are international in scope.

The amount of information available on the internet is almost limitless. For example, the Monica Lewinsky–Bill Clinton scandal was first brought into the public domain on the internet. Only then did newspapers take up the story. At the time of going to press with this book, public interest is still intense (see Figure 4.4), and one website shows no fewer than twenty thousand entries!

Another useful internet source is the PRnet Newswire (Figure 4.5), which stores press releases.

Radio on the internet

You can also listen to and download sound versions of the news through Live Radio on the Internet (Figure 4.6) website. With a click of the mouse, you select radio stations worldwide. IRN is there too (Figure 4.7), and is updated automatically.

Radio web sites are:

- IRN: http://www.irn.co.uk
- Radio stations: http://www.frodo.u-net.com/
- Radio stations: http://wmbr.mit.edu/stations/list.html

Newspapers and magazines on the internet

Newspapers usually provide free access to articles for one month; after this articles move to the archive section and can only be accessed for a fee (Figure 4.8).

The web site to consult is: http://www.mediainfo.com

Reference books and sources

One of the essential attributes of any journalist is to know where to get information. Apart from sources such as the internet, all journal-

34 A Guide to Commercial Radio Journalism

Figure 4.2 Yahoo! website on the internet

Webcrawler Top Stories News

news channel
home · my page · email · help
-- Choose a Channel --

Click Here!

News | Business | Sports | Entertainment | Sci-Tech | Nation | World | Health

Web Site Guide

Broadcast News
Business
Columns
Current Events
Entertainment
Journalism
Magazines
News Services
Sports
Technology
U.S. Newspapers
Weather
World Newspapers

Ongoing Coverage

Apple's New iMac
Astrology & Horoscopes
Astronomy News

Capitol Hill Shooting
Celebrity Gossip
Clinton Sex Scandal

Crime & Criminals
Diana Remembered
Litigation & Lawsuits

Microsoft Fights DOJ
Movie News & Reviews
NASA's Space Missions

Nuclear Bomb Testing
Rock & Roll News
Russian Economic Woes

Showdown with Iraq
Small Business Update
Summer Heat Waves

Tabloid.net News
Tobacco Settlement?
U.S. Strikes Back

Viagra, Miracle Drug?
Weather Watcher

Top Story Headlines

Last Update: 04:21 PM ET 08/31/98

Viktor Chernomyrdin Speaks (Reuters)

Russian Duma Rejects Chernomyrdin

Russia's State Duma has rejected the appointment of Viktor Chernomyrdin as new Russian prime minister, voting 251-94 against President Boris Yeltsin's candidate.

Headlines from Reuters and UPI

Dow in second largest drop in history
WWII survivors sue VW for 'slave' wages
Hutchison pushes for missile defense
Northwest strike looms into Labor Day weekend
Experts say fat rivals smoking as health threat

Hurricane Danielle stronger, no threat to land
Britain remembers Diana with flowers and prayers
N. Korea launches missile over Japan
More embassy bombing suspects to be sent to U.S.
Russian parliament rejects Yeltsin's prime minister

Sen. Lott says Clinton sets 'tragic example'
Clinton says West should help Russia if it reforms
School noted for early integration
Top mediator talks to Northwest, pilots
Ohio nun to serve 14-month prison term

Dollar pressured by Wall Street
American returns to Love Field
NAM calls on Fed to cut rates
Justices honor Powell at funeral
Woman mum on selling donated horses

http://nt.excite.com/webcrawler/   31/08/98

Figure 4.3 WebCrawler news page on the internet

36 A Guide to Commercial Radio Journalism

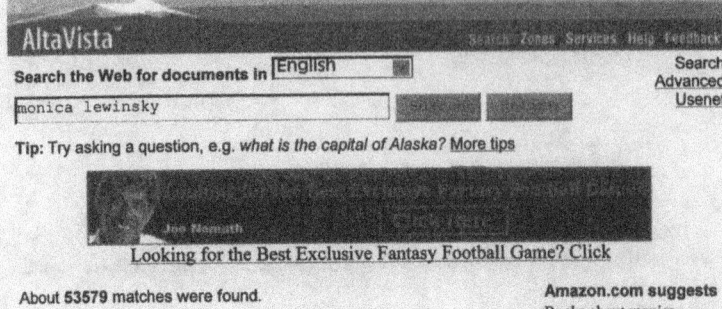

Figure 4.4 The Bill Clinton–Monica Lewinsky affair on the internet

Finding the story   37

PRnet Press Release Search   Page 1 of 1

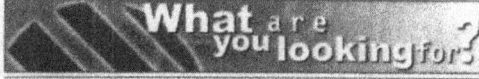

home

search

This page allows you, as a journalist, to access all the very latest press releases on PRnet, without any limitations. For quick, easy access to breaking news, take a look at all the new press releases in the last 24 hours. To display press releases targeted at various areas, take a look at our categorised searches. Alternatively, use our keyword search to get specific information about a particular topic, whether that is a company or product, or anything else more general.

configure

Display all the press releases that have arrived in the past 24 hours.

View press releases by region.

Show press releases categorised into areas of interest.

contacts

Search for press releases using keywords, company names or product names.

feedback

Search for companies in the PRnet Press Contacts database.

help

Root | Home | Search | Contacts | Feedback | Help | Copyright

If you have any comments or suggestions about these pages, please feel free to contact the webmaster, fill in our on-line feedback form, or call PRnet support directly on 01604 672004.

http://www.prnet.co.uk/Journalists/search.html   25/04/98

Figure 4.5 The PRnet press release service on the internet

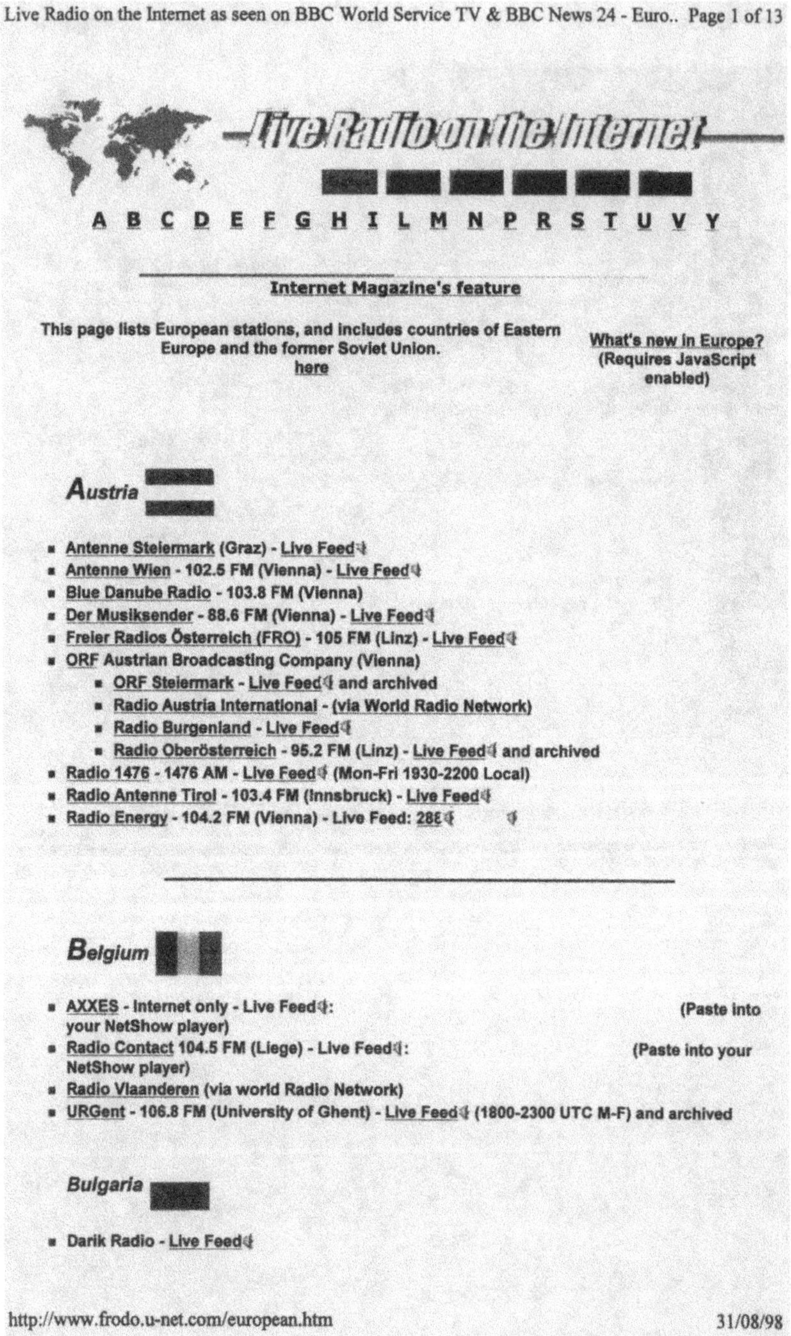

Live Radio on the Internet as seen on BBC World Service TV & BBC News 24 - Euro.. Page 1 of 13

Live Radio on the Internet

A B C D E F G H I L M N P R S T U V Y

Internet Magazine's feature

This page lists European stations, and includes countries of Eastern Europe and the former Soviet Union.
here

What's new in Europe?
(Requires JavaScript enabled)

Austria

- Antenne Steiermark (Graz) - Live Feed
- Antenne Wien - 102.5 FM (Vienna) - Live Feed
- Blue Danube Radio - 103.8 FM (Vienna)
- Der Musiksender - 88.6 FM (Vienna) - Live Feed
- Freier Radios Österreich (FRO) - 105 FM (Linz) - Live Feed
- ORF Austrian Broadcasting Company (Vienna)
  - ORF Steiermark - Live Feed and archived
  - Radio Austria International - (via World Radio Network)
  - Radio Burgenland - Live Feed
  - Radio Oberösterreich - 95.2 FM (Linz) - Live Feed and archived
- Radio 1476 - 1476 AM - Live Feed (Mon-Fri 1930-2200 Local)
- Radio Antenne Tirol - 103.4 FM (Innsbruck) - Live Feed
- Radio Energy - 104.2 FM (Vienna) - Live Feed: 28S

Belgium

- AXXES - Internet only - Live Feed: (Paste into your NetShow player)
- Radio Contact 104.5 FM (Liege) - Live Feed: (Paste into your NetShow player)
- Radio Vlaanderen (via world Radio Network)
- URGent - 106.8 FM (University of Ghent) - Live Feed (1800-2300 UTC M-F) and archived

Bulgaria

- Darik Radio - Live Feed

http://www.frodo.u-net.com/european.htm   31/08/98

Figure 4.6 How to find broadcast stations on the internet

Finding the story **39**

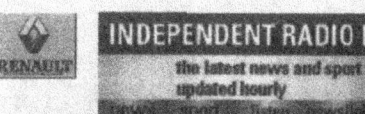 

Hear the 22:00 IRN bulletin in RealAudio at 14.4 or 28.8 kbps
(bulletins are available approximately ten minutes after the hour)

    28.8

Check the classified football results (during the season) from
Saturday 29/08/98

 28.8

If you haven't got it, you'll need to download the RealPlayer.

Our RealAudio server has moved. If you included a direct link to
the file on your home page please check the revised details. If you
experience any problems with RealAudio at IRN please contact our
RealAudio Administrator.

| news | sport | listen | newslink | reader | about IRN |

© 1997 IRN and individual contributors. All rights reserved.
Site management by Satellite Media Services

http://www.irn.co.uk/listen.html   31/08/98

Figure 4.7 IRN radio website

Figure 4.8 Website of *The Daily Telegraph*

ists should make themselves familiar with reference books.
Useful Search Engines on the internet include:

- Yahoo (http://www.yahoo.co.uk); has the largest database
- Alta Vista (http://www.alta vista.com)
- HotBot (http://www.hotbot.com)
- Excite (http://www.excite.com); extra depth
- InfoSeek (http://www.infoseek.com)
- DejaNews (http://www.dejanews.com); this is the best source for news groups, i.e., where groups of people interested about selected topics exchange information. News groups can provide unexpected and interesting information amongst much egocentric dross.

Information about the United Kingdom in particular can be found from directories like:

- The Internet Directory UK (http://www.internet-directory.co.uk)
- UK Yellow Pages (http://www.yell.co.uk)

Other reference sources include:

- CD-ROMs: most encyclopaedias and dictionaries (Encyclopaedia Britannica, Encarta, Grolier etc.) and a host of other sources can be found on CD-ROMs and cost much less than the book version. Consult the Yahoo website, among others, for lists of CD-ROM publishers.
- *Who's Who* lists people in the UK country whom the editors have decided are important. The entries are in alphabetical order and are based on information supplied by the entrants themselves. Each entry gives a summary of the person's career and interests, as well as who they are married to, how many children they have, etc. It also gives some kind of contact point (a club or sometimes a home address and phone number).
- *Current Biography* contains short and medium length articles on prominent people and is also available on CD-ROM.
- *Debrett's Prominent People* is similar to *Who's Who* but has more home telephone numbers.
- *International Who's Who* covers people who are well known internationally, and is compiled on the same basis as *Who's Who*.
- *Dod's Parliamentary Companion* lists all the current members of Parliament sitting in both the Commons and the Lords. It will tell you when they entered Parliament, what posts they hold or have held, and which issues they are particularly interested in. There are other good Parliamentary guides, but Dod's is among those with a reputation for accuracy. All the political parties have their own websites.

- *Directory of British Associations* is a gem. It lists almost every association in the country which is not a government body or quango, giving details of the purpose of the organisation, who is in charge and the address and phone number. It includes everybody from AAA (Action Against Allergy) to the Zip Manufacturers Association (with apologies to the Zoological Societies of Glasgow and London).
- *British Books in Print* lists every book currently in print in the UK. It is cross-referenced according to subject, title and author. It can be a starting point for finding an expert in a particular field, but you will not be able to tell what any author's prejudice may be.
- *Contemporary Authors* has articles of varying length according to the views of the editors. It also contains bibliographies and, journalists-in-a-hurry take note, interviews with some of the authors.
- *Willing's Press Guide* lists all the newspapers and journals registered in Britain and has an international section as well. It can help you find a contact in a specialised field. The Guide also lists the internet addresses of newspapers and magazines that have websites.
- *Statesman's Year Book* can make you an instant expert on any country with which Britain has diplomatic relations. It gives a short history of each country, a summary of the economy, something about the major cities and some geography, as well as listing the names of the diplomatic personnel and the telephone number of the British embassy or mission.
- *Guinness Book of Records*: the index at the back will direct you to your subject.
- *Screen International Film and TV Yearbook* lists actors, producers, directors, etc., and all the films or programmes they have been involved in.
- *International Film Encyclopaedia* (ed. Katz): all the entries are based on people, events etc. in film, e.g. the 'Italy' entry gives that country's history in the film industry.
- *Halliwell's Film Guide* covers more than 15,000 films and tells you what each film was about, who wrote it, starred in it and sometimes what the critics said about it. You may not agree with Leslie Halliwell's opinions, but he will tell you just about anything you need to know about a film.
- *International Dictionary of Films and Filmmakers* has extensive articles and filmographies in four separate volumes on Films, Directors, Actors, Writers.
- Internet – Movie Database: http://www.allmovie.com
- Internet – All Movie Guide: http://us.imdb.com
- *Oxford Companion to the Theatre,* like the film encyclopaedia, lists people, events etc. based on the theatre.

- *International Dictionary of the Theatre*: has extensive articles on playwrights and artists and actors.
- *Music Master* and *MM Track Index*: *Music Master* lists international singers or groups alphabetically and all the albums or singles they have recorded; the *Track Index* is an alphabetical list of song titles and who recorded them.
- *Guinness British Hit Singles* is split into three sections: the first two are alphabetical listings of artists and titles, the third part lists 'Facts and Feats', including 'Most Weeks in Chart' and 'Least Successful Chart Act'.
- Internet – All Music Guide: http://www.allmusic.com
- Internet – Classical Music: http://www.classical.net
- *Oxford Dictionary of Quotations* lists well-known quotations. Useful if you want to quote accurately, check who said it, or find an appropriate quotation. If, for instance, you want a quote with the word 'write' in it, you will be directed to Shakespeare's 'have to write me down an ass'. You would find the same quote under 'ass'.
- *Whitaker's Almanac*, a reference source which you must already know.
- *The Knowledge*, a database of media-related companies and professionals.

Archive sources

Many newsrooms keep a library of newspaper cuttings, which are a good source of recent stories and profiles of the famous. Always photocopy the cuttings you want to use and return the originals.

Similarly, if a tape archive section is kept, dub off any interview or the part of it that you want to use and replace the tape in its box in its full form. Never cut any part of an archive tape!

CHAPTER 5

Telling the story

Reporting

Getting that exclusive interview or digging up a story that causes a crisis in government is every reporter's dream, but even the most experienced investigative reporter does not stumble over such gems every day, and no sensational story is ever a gift. Hard work, determination and attention to detail lie behind every big story. We all learn to take short-cuts, but it is important to be aware of the dangers of taking them. So learn the craft well and build up a good solid background.

A good reporter will always find out from the editor or producer what angle is required, how long the piece should run, and when it is needed. These three items of information must be the first you ascertain. They may be obvious, but if ever you are not sure, it doesn't matter how busy the editor or producer is, find out. Otherwise you will almost certainly waste time chasing the wrong angle.

The other essential quality of any good reporter is knowing that anything can be a story and being keen to get it. A good reporter will do as good a job putting together a piece about a siege as one about the awarding of the title 'Loo of the Year'.

There was once an editor at IRN who had a gift for convincing reporters that if they 'did this one right' it could lead the bulletin. The wonderful thing was, even duff stories often ended up being well placed! Install a bit of that editor in your mind. Aim to make every piece you do worthy of being the lead.

Contacts

Every journalist needs to keep comprehensive list of contacts. An electronic personal organiser or contacts book is almost always the first stage of getting to a story, and being able to get to the right person fast is all-important. Back up your entries or take photocopies of each page of your contacts book regularly so that if it is lost you are not left wanting your right arm.

NB: Electronic organisers can crash; so always back up your contacts. I have known an editor lose about twenty years' worth of contacts in this way.

If you have a memory like a sieve, work out a way of cross-indexing your contacts so that you can find numbers quickly. One system is to divide each letter of the alphabet into three sections: **people**, **organisations** and **subjects**. Then, if a story breaks in India, for example, you can turn to the subjects section under 'I' and find a list of people and organisations with expert knowledge of India. If you use a loose-leaf binder, it will be easier to add pages to sections that become full, or replace pages that become largely redundant.

News releases and embargoes

If you are doing a story from a news release, your job will be made that little bit easier. The release will not only sell you the story (without necessarily telling you the whole tale), it will also give you contact names and numbers.

The contacts are normally PRs, who are almost never the right people to talk to. They are not decision-makers but information disseminators. They are therefore most unlikely to be able to answer questions such as 'What are you going to do about it?' Go for the person at the top.

Try not to waste time by letting people say they will ring you back. Tell them you will hold on. This demonstrates that you are serious, and that you think they are important. Moreover, phones have a compulsive quality: how many people do you know who ignore a ringing telephone just because they are involved in an important conversation?

If you are trying to get someone to come in to the studio, or if the person you want to talk to is not around or difficult to get to, then you may have to wait for a call back. Just be aware that you are putting yourself in their hands rather than being in control yourself.

The news release may carry an 'embargo', which is a request to hold publication of the information until a particular date and time. An embargo is sometimes included for practical and sensible reasons, such as when it is timed to a particular event or the publication of a report. At other times it is difficult to see the sense of an embargo, and it may be that the organisers are trying to manipulate the timing for their own reasons. For example, it is well known within the industry that Mondays are 'bad news' days because fewer newsworthy events tend to happen on Sunday. Therefore items that would probably not get a look-in most other days just might 'make' on a Monday.

Embargoes carry no statutory weight, although there might be a case for a breach of copyright claim in some circumstances. So far as I know, however, no one has brought such a case. When an embargo is broken the more usual remedy is an internal one within the industry, such as withdrawing facilities.

For example, the Queen's Honours List always comes out in advance under a 'strict embargo' so that we can organise pre-recorded interviews with people on the list and have coverage ready as soon as the embargo comes off. Until 1987 no one ever broke the embargo. Then the *Sun* ran a story on two Zeebrugge heroes who were to receive the George Medal the day before the New Year Honours list came off embargo. Since then the Palace has released the names just twelve hours before the embargo rather than giving the two days' advance notice we used to get.

Government department embargoes are seldom broken, but since politicians can be nearly as cynical as journalists, big announcements are often preceded only by a terse invitation to a news conference, just in case. If you are faced with such an invitation, it is worth ringing the department's press office. They will sometimes tell you over the phone what they are not willing to put on paper; at the very least, you should be able to find out whether it is going to be an important announcement that needs to be covered.

If you want to break an embargo, you will usually have to get the originator's agreement in order to get any actuality. That is one of the drawbacks of radio. If a newspaper breaks an embargo, on the other hand, broadcasters must either chase the story at double speed or ditch it; if it is in the papers the listener may think we are a day behind. If the story is still worth telling, at least any resistance will have been broken down by the paper's report.

Sourcing

One of the rules of reporting is that every story should be 'double sourced'. This is vital when using material from the internet. If a dependable reporter has not seen or heard something first hand, get confirmation of the facts from another source before running it. This may be difficult, but it is one of the times when you must employ the 'if in doubt, leave it out' rule. A good story may be knocking about, but if you cannot harden it up it is dangerous to run it.

If the first you hear of a story is when it comes up on the wires, still check it. Our colleagues in all the major services are first-rate, but even the best of us can make mistakes, and the story may have moved on since the reporter filed the copy. But, more important, this is radio. Copy filed on the wires will at least have to be rewritten before it is voiced up, but we need more. We need actuality and colour!

Tip-offs

Tip-offs can be useful, whether from freelances (whom you have to pay) or from listeners (who are not as reliable). In either case, check the information before you go to air with it. There are a lot of hoaxers out there who get a kick out of tricking new organisations and planting false stories. So be careful to verify all tip-offs.

If you get a tip-off from a listener, thank the person politely but treat the information warily. You are there to get the facts right; moreover what the listener thinks is news may not fit in with the newsroom's definition. Having said that, if it is important to one person, it may be worth checking to see if it has wider appeal. If it is a major local story that you are not on top of, hop to it. You are already late off the mark!

Check calls

One of the most important ways of staying on top of 'your patch' is to contact the emergency services regularly. These are known as check calls, and reporters should be in touch with fire, ambulance and police every couple of hours. That is the theory, but like everything else in life the practice may be more complicated.

In larger cities, the emergency services' press rooms often have a taped version of what is happening which press officers will update on a more or less regular basis. Depending on what sort of day it is, or who the press officer is, the tape may be updated less frequently than we would like. The person designated to deal with check calls is not at the scene and may not know the story, let alone the latest. Trying to go directly to the person dealing with an incident as it is happening could make you very unpopular, and ancillary staff may not know what is going on. Be guided by press officers or their subordinates, but remember that there is no substitute for getting to the scene.

At the scene

Once you are there, find out who is in charge and whether anyone else has been designated to keep you informed. Position yourself so that you can see the event (without putting yourself at any risk; a hospitalised reporter is of little use to the newsdesk), and keep your recorder running, doing commentaries from the scene regularly to update the desk and for possible use later in a wrap. There is almost nothing more frustrating than to be on the scene and miss the actuality of an explosion, gun fire or angry exchange because you were 'resting' your recorder.

Do not get in the way of the emergency services, but do not be a lamb either. There are situations in which the police will keep you out of the line of sight, e.g. at major sieges where firearms are involved, but they happen very rarely.

Door-stepping

'Door-stepping' is the bane of reporters, but essential to getting certain sorts of stories. There you are in the pouring rain, sitting outside the area that is meant to produce your story; the newsdesk keeps nagging you for an update even though nothing has moved; there is nowhere to get a snack for lunch, let alone a toilet; and you and all the other journos are getting very fed up. Fight boredom. When the story breaks, you will have to respond quickly; if you have become lethargic your poor reaction time may cost you that moment of perfect actuality.

Think about your positioning. For instance, if a celebrity arrives at Heathrow Airport, you should work out where they will probably emerge and position yourself to beat the pack. Newspaper journalists often carry little tape recorders in order to ensure they get the quote right, but they do not have to have broadcast quality. Get your microphone in front of the person who matters – somehow. If you are tall you may be able to reach over other people's shoulders, or if you are small, under their armpits. You may just have to imagine you are on the Tokyo tube and squeeze yourself into a non-existent space. Get there. What is the point of undergoing all those tedious hours just to go back to the desk to tell them your actuality is not broadcastable?

News conferences

The other situation in which you must get your mike in the right place is the news conference. Don't forget the mike stand. If more than one person is making a statement, don't be shy about getting to the table and moving your mike. News conferences are also called press conferences, and while we in radio prefer the word news (we don't like being left out), these conferences are designed for print journalists.

Supplementary questions from the pack will be off-mike and unusable, which means you will have to wrap it.

Sometimes the actuality from the conference is all you need, or all you can get, but it is usually better to arrange in advance to get your own interview or 'Q & A' afterwards. Press the PR or whoever is making arrangements to let you nip in before the TV people. Their equipment takes time to rig up and their interviews take longer to do. They also have to shoot 'cut-aways' or 'noddies' in order to disguise a film edit. By the time they have finished you will probably have missed at least one bulletin, and if there is more than one TV crew around, you will be cooling your heels for quite a while. PRs like getting their story on TV and usually consider it more important than radio, so use the immediacy of radio to get your place in front. 'My editor really wants this story for the next bulletin' flatters them.

Government ministers and some other high-ranking people ask for an advance list of the questions you will ask in the interview. Keep to areas rather than specific questions, and remember the phrase 'plus supplementaries'. Without that phrase, some interviewees can get rather prickly about answering anything but the exact subject areas you said you were going to cover, so if they drop a bombshell in one of their answers, they will stall answering your pick-up questions (or even downright refuse).

Sometimes interviewees ask for an advance list when it is not really justified. Tell them politely that it is just a straightforward interview covering the general issues. Giving an advance list not only restricts you, it is also time-consuming, and a radio reporter should always be aware of the clock's relentless second hand.

Pressure groups

These are another major source of news. They range from the 'worthies' to political and trade unions, and they all have an axe to grind. Often you will find it of interest to your listener to help them at the grindstone, but do not let a bit of panic about filling your air-time influence your decision. You should be able to take a more creative approach, like finding that extra angle on a good story.

Silly seasons

All this may sound as though there are always stories just waiting to be tackled. If only that were true. Of course there are days when good stories stream in and you have to deal with two or three at once. You end up working overtime and go home exhausted but satisfied.

But there is also the silly season. This phrase used to be reserved for the summer (mainly August), but now it is often used to cover any of those times when the only things moving are departing holidaymakers. Parliament, local councils and the courts are major sources of news, and they all take breaks not only in the summer, but also around Christmas and Easter. At such times, even if there is a breaking story, there may well be nobody around to talk about it. This is when a good contacts book and your local knowledge become your life-lines.

Interviewing

Interviews on radio carry a stronger impact than those in the press, because the listener often deduces as much information from how a question is answered as from the actual words spoken. If the interviewee hesitates before answering, that pause may tell the listener at least as much as the words that eventually follow.

Your job is to get the interviewee to divulge facts, reasons or opinions. Do not forget the basic rule that your opinions simply do not matter. You need to do your homework before the interview and listen carefully while it is going on, but your opinions must not get in the way.

The first kind of interview a story is likely to require is the straightforward informative sort. When a story first breaks, you need to find out exactly what has happened. You may be just as much in the dark as the listener, and your questions will flow from a natural inquisitiveness or from the interviewee's replies. If, for example, there has been a major fire at a chemical plant, the senior fire officer may be interviewed about how it started, whether there is a danger to residents in the area, etc. But if, during the course of the interview, it emerges that this particular plant has had a series of fires, the interview may change direction.

At that point, the fire officer may be asked interpretative questions, such as whether fire safety regulations had been observed or whether they are good enough. Interpretative interviews are trying to get behind the facts so that the listener can put the issue into perspective. It could be anything from asking the Chancellor why interest rates had to go up to why a particular performance by a ballet company did not come up to scratch.

The most difficult kind of interview to do is the emotional. If their children have been killed in school by a deranged gunman, it is an intrusion to ask mothers and fathers and families how they feel. It is not just an intrusion on them, it also intrudes on the listener. Emotional interviews convey the human side of a story, and sharing an experience is an important part of life that has its place. You must, though, put yourself in the place of the interviewee. 'When did you first hear about the shootings' is a more appropriate question. The stress and worry will come through. Or at the other end of the scale, delight and relief will come across once 'all the men are found safe'. It is when the emotion is pleasurable that it is appropriate to ask 'How do you feel?'

The personality interview, on the other hand, is meant to be entertaining and revealing. It usually involves a celebrity, but can extend to anyone well-known, from politicians to union leaders. The basis of the interview is always the person rather than an event. Be sensitive when the interview strays into emotional areas. The interviewee may start talking about how drugs or drink was a problem at some time, or the effect of the death of someone close. It is an important part of that person's life, and therefore belongs in the interview, but find a way of bringing the interview back to positive aspects in order to end on a high note.

If you are going for this sort of interview, be sure that the interviewee knows what you want. Some people in the public eye resent probing questions about their private lives.

The RA lays down these four basic guidelines for all interviews:

- If a person is interviewed as a representative of an organisation or group, you must be sure that the person is entitled to speak on its behalf.
- The interviewee must be told how the interview will be used.
- The interviewee must be told the identity and role of any other participants in the wrap or programme.
- If the interview takes place over the phone, you must be sure that the interviewee knows it is being recorded for possible transmission.

Remember that you are asking the questions on behalf of the listener. You have access to more information, so you may ask questions the listener would not have thought of, but in the end you need to get across the information the listener not only wants to know, but should know.

An interview must be spontaneous, so, discuss the general areas that will be covered beforehand without revealing the actual questions. Interviewees will start contriving their answers if they know the actual questions, or, worse, decide to make notes on what they want to say. The result will be a stilted interview that might as well appear in a newspaper.

If you are turned down for an interview, be careful of using the 'No comment' phrase. It can imply that there is something to hide. If someone does not want to react to a report until there has been time to read it, or management does not want to respond to union allegations until there has been a meeting, say so. If the phrase was 'There's no comment at this time', are you giving the listener an accurate reflection if you leave off the last three words? If the answer to that is yes, then go ahead, but consider it first.

When preparing for an interview, you must be clear why you are doing it and what you expect to come out of it. The first half of that equation is usually easier than the second. Do as much research as you can or have time for, because if the interviewee comes up with something startling and you do not understand the background well enough to recognise it, the listener will quite rightly be annoyed.

Some of that research may well involve going back over newspaper clippings. Use the information you find there, but always check it. It may have been wrong in the first place; even if it was accurate, things may have changed since then. Where possible, talk to the person concerned, or their press officer or agent, beforehand to make sure your information is up to date.

All this assumes you have any time at all. If it is a breaking story, you will have to emulate the emergency services. Get to the scene fast and hope that the information you carry in your head will be good enough in the first instance. That means staying on top of the news and knowing which angles or issues are contentious. If a plane crashes, you need to know whether that particular type of aircraft has been involved in a string of crashes without spending valuable time having to look it up. Most editors expect reporters to have read at least one serious and one popular newspaper each day, and to have seen at least one of the major television news broadcasts.

Before you start any interview, ascertain the basic facts. You must get names, positions and dates right. The interviewee will be irritated if you get them wrong, and if you are constantly having to be corrected over minor matters the main thrust of the interview will be lost.

Talk to the interviewee beforehand to find out what sort of talker he or she is and clarify any facts that you are not sure about. You may also need to calm down nervous people or encourage timid ones. Be straight with people, but do not reveal your punchlines if it is not an informational interview. You can tell someone what areas you plan to cover without giving away your line of attack.

If the interview is to be live, telling the guest the gist of the first question may start it off more smoothly. If it is a prerecorded interview, the first question should really end up as part of the cue material, or may be designed to put the interviewee at ease – in either case expect the first question and answer to be cut. It can, however, be a useful double-check on levels. People often speak at a different level when they know the machine is recording.

A good interview will cover the '5 Ws and H':

- Who?
- When?
- What?
- How?
- Where?
- Why?

The only one that does not ask for a fact or an interpretation of a fact is 'Why?', often the most important question because it asks for an opinion or reason and usually provokes the most interesting response. By the time you have finished your report, all six questions should have been answered either in the interview itself or in a combination of cue and interview.

Avoid closed questions that start with 'will', 'is', 'did' or 'have' unless you want a single-word answer. You may want to provoke a yes/no reply to vary the pace of the interview or emphasise a particular point. Just know the danger of what you are doing, and be ready with the follow-up question.

Your questions should be clear and simple. Use as few words as you can, and include just one concept per question. Do not make statements unless they are carefully couched; there is a danger of them pulling you out of the objective role. Put the other side of the argument, but do not let it sound like your opinion. Attribute the other side if you can ('The leader of the opposition says the Council is over-spent'); even if it is a general point, distance yourself from it ('Some people may say that the Council is over-spent').

Your questions should progress in a logical way. If you are going to change direction, sign-post the change: 'On a different issue altogether, Councillor, you've been quoted as saying ...'

Questions should be neither too broad (What did you find in your six-month study tour?') nor too narrow ('And how long did little Alice cry after she fell over?').

Use general questions ('Can you summarise for the listeners what has happened?') when you, perhaps, have not had time to research a subject. It will help you become aware of events. But it can give the interviewees the impression that you are not briefed on the subject and allows them to control, at least, the beginning of the interview. A good reporter will use the answer to this question for information and cue and will quickly regain control.

Never ask leading questions. By definition, they take you out of your objective role. Remember that you are getting the facts, information or opinions of others so that listeners can formulate their own conclusions. For the same reason, avoid adjectives and adverbs. It is up to the listener to decide whether a 50 per cent increase is large.

Mind your manners. A 'hard' interview is not necessarily aggressive. There are times when an interview becomes adversarial, but the listener should be able to follow why it has done so. You will generally get more out of an interview if you use polite but dogged persistence.

On the other side of the coin, a lot of inexperienced reporters find it difficult to pluck up the courage to ask any questions, even easy ones. It is unnatural to ask prying questions of a perfect stranger, so it is not surprising that many beginners worry about how they are going to perform.

Find a formula for settling your nerves. You must always respect the position of the interviewee, but remember that the interview would not be happening if there had not been an agreement for it to take place.

If you want to include a 'tough' question, do not put it first or leave it till last. Put it in about third or fourth – by then the interviewee's guard may be down, and there is still time for follow-up questions if it proves an interesting answer.

If an interviewee responds to a question with a question, never answer it. Press for a proper answer if it is needed, but if the question is rhetorical, let the listener answer it while you move on to another area of questioning. Sometimes rhetorical questions can make a good end to an interview.

Use your eyes and facial expression to register understanding, avoiding annoying vocal interjections. Small noises of agreement, unnoticeable in ordinary conversation, can be intensely annoying for the listener.

Be aware of what the interviewee is wearing. Bracelets that jangle or leather jackets that squeak may be very fashionable, but that is not a major consideration on the radio.

If you are doing an interview out in the field, arrange yourself and the interviewee in a sort of V design if you can, because then you can keep both of you on mike without having to move it as much as if you were face to face. Never let an interviewee sit on the other side of a desk. Even if you have arms the length of a gorilla's, the mike lead will suffer from whip-lash and your arm will ache.

Always listen to what the interviewee is saying and pick up on it with supplementary questions if necessary. If the interview starts to drift, bring it back on course. Do not allow jargon or technical terms to go unexplained. When you are getting near the end of the interview, please do not say '... and finally...'. I have edited tapes that contained as many as three 'and finally's' and have heard presenters do the same on live interviews.

Finish the interview on a high note. People tend to remember what they hear first and last, so make both ends sparkle.

Once you have done the interview, do not let the interviewee listen to it. People tend to want to change something. If you are happy with the interview, that is good enough. The only other people who matter at this stage are the editor and the listener.

Story presentation

Your method of presentation may be dictated by the nature of the story or simply by the deadline. Constraints of time may rule out the ideal.

News cuts

The simplest mode of presentation is the news cut, which runs in short news bulletins. That only requires choosing the best short clip of the interview, which could be as short as 5 seconds, or as long as the house style of the station allows, which in IRN's case is 15 seconds. This sounds deceptively simple: remember that the clip must add to the story, be understandable and self-contained, and that the inflections have to be right.

A news cut can also be 'wrapped', with two clips of actuality both introduced and linked by a reporter. Since it still has to be short, the clips will almost certainly be around 10 seconds.

In programme terms, your choice of presentation is broader.

Question and answer (Q & A)

These were traditionally interviews with reporters at the scene of a story, who either hot-foot it into the studio to tell the tale before processing actuality, or explain what is happening from the scene, live on air. The phrase is now often used to describe any interview.

Phone-outs

When a story first breaks, the fastest way to cover it will almost certainly be by telephone. There are other times when phone interviews may be unavoidable, perhaps because the story is happening in a remote area or there is no time to get good quality lines organised. But the simplicity and time-saving qualities of the phone-out may tempt you to use it too often, without considering its disadvantages. The phone line quality makes it that much more difficult for the listener to concentrate on the information. If it is a live phone-out, there is also a danger that the line will deteriorate during the course of the interview. The loss of eye contact can be an added disadvantage, because a person's demeanour can suggest a lot to the interviewer.

If you must cover a story by phone, keep the interview as short as you can while still giving all the essential information. Most producers will only accept a phone quality interview on a local story if it is a major story and there is no other way of covering it. It should be approached as a holding operation that informs the listener quickly. Every effort should be made to get good quality actuality back to base as fast as possible.

Wraps

Most stories have at least two sides to them, and you should present a balanced and comprehensive report. This could be achieved by running a series of Q & As, but that is very time-consuming and probably the least interesting way of presenting a story.

A much better way is to pre-record interviews with all the necessary people and then 'wrap it'. Wraps are the most creative form of presentation, and you can really pack a lot of information into them. While one question and its answer might take a minute of air time, you can get two sides of an issue, plus an explanation of what is going on, into the same amount of time in a wrap.

You can mix sound effects, music and several different participants in your report. Wraps take longer to put together than Q & As, but are a far better listen. You can compress or paraphrase someone's argument, and just use the startling or interesting bit. There may be times when you are unable to get an interview, but the necessary information can be scripted into the wrap so that the report is still fair and balanced.

The interview may happen in a noisy place such as a reception with people talking in the background. Always record at least five minutes wild-tracking, i.e. the sound of the atmospherics at the location of the interview. When you are putting the wrap together in the studio, you can then run the wild-track behind your voice so there is no sudden change of quality. If there does need to be a change in background sounds, let the track run under your voice for a few seconds before fading it out, and then fade in the next track before the next bit of actuality. In that way you can take the listener with you from one location to another.

Put the components of the wrap in separate bands, so that you can be flexible when deciding the order in which they should appear in the script, and they can be played in without the need to edit gaps when the wrap is being recorded.

An adaptation of the wrap is the 'linked story' – a short interview with one person as the first band, and another as the second band, leaving the presenter to link the two live on air.

Vox pops

Vox pops, from the Latin *vox populi* ('voice of the people'), can be lively, interesting little pieces, but you should take care when deciding which issues make good vox pop candidates.

Vox pops are put together by going out on the street to elicit people's opinions on a subject, then editing them together in sequence so that the question appears only in the cue. They should never be presented as a representative sample. Apart from the obvious fact that you are not presenting a scientifically based report, the whole idea is to pick out the most interesting or lively comments without entirely distorting the general trend of the replies.

The question that elicits the replies must be thought through so that it is easy for people to understand and does not offer them the option of answering with a simple 'yes' or 'no'. If, for example, a report has been published which claims managers are hiring older secretaries who have a wealth of experience rather than attractive young women who can supply cups of tea, a question asking why people think this is happening is better than one asking do people believe it. Or your question can indicate a more light-hearted approach, such as 'When do you think it appropriate for a manager to make the tea rather than the secretary?'

When the recordings are being made, ask the questions with the recorder on pause and only record people's answers. When the vox is being put together, put the replies you want to use into separate bands or carts so that you can start and finish with the best answers. Make those in the middle a good mix of opinions, varying between male and female voices if possible.

Some producers consider that vox pops are a simple and straightforward way to cover a story. They are wrong. Vox pops take up a lot of the reporter's time, are suited mostly for light items and for fewer issues than you might imagine.

News presentation

When a story breaks it must be covered. Major stories have a habit of breaking just before bulletins or the start of programmes, forcing you to stretch your resources, skills and intelligence to get them to air fast but accurately.

Remember that three words equal 1 second. A 3 minute bulletin equals 540 words – not a lot, which is why IRN has the general rule that cuts have to be a maximum of 30 seconds and wraps no more than 35. Fitting a complex story into 35 seconds will certainly stretch a reporter's writing skills, but spare a thought for the scriptwriter who has to get the story into a two-line headline. Listen to reports on radio and television and analyse the reporters' styles. It will teach you a great deal.

Updating a story is different from 'freshening it up'. Updating involves new material which takes the story further. Freshening is re-writing the same material so it does not sound stale, or presenting an alternative aspect, either in script or in actuality.

Our job is to convey information clearly and in a way that the listener will understand and want to hear. If we use exactly the same words hour after hour, the listener will become bored and switch off, so freshening up or updating stories is an important part of the job.

News bulletins and news programmes

Journalists who work on the news desk and put together bulletins have the same qualifications as those who work on news programme desks, but they deal with stories differently. For a start, they will have a different idea of who the listener is; in IRN's case, the editors must not think in terms of any particular local audience, even though the bulletin originates from London. It is a national service, so the bulletin has to fit into the programme formats of ILR stations around the country, and the stories must be relevant to everyone.

If a bulletin is a local one, the editor's choice of stories and story order may reflect that to some degree, but the bulletin will still not necessarily sound the same as a news programme. Bulletins are a summary of the news and, in IRN's case, the majority of them must pack the international and national news into 3 minutes. News programmes, on the other hand, can devote more time to explaining the details or background to a story. Even if the format of the programme does not allow items to exceed 3½ minutes, that still constitutes more time than the whole of most IRN bulletins.

Partly because of these considerations, there is also a difference in basic news judgements. A bulletin may well lead on events in the United States on the same day as a news programme leads on the announcement of new rail links for the area. Both stories may feature in both bulletins and the programme, but each has different priorities, and the placement of the stories will reflect that.

While a bulletin will cover international news, the listener expects a local station to present relevant weather and travel information as well as the local news – indeed, that is one of the strengths of local radio.

There are also differences in style. Even if the same presenter is reading a bulletin and then going on to front a programme, the bulletin will tend to be read straight, without comment or personality. Once the programme gets under way, the presenter's personality and style not only can but must come through.

News judgement

Deciding which items to include in a news bulletin and in what order, or 'news judgement', is largely instinctive and subjective, based on the culture of a newsroom and the perceived audience. While the editors at IRN might each write up a story differently, they would usually agree on the order, or at least the lead story.

The death of Princess Diana is a good example. Such a major story often completely takes over a bulletin when it first breaks, then dominates bulletins as it moves along, disappearing days later. It will reappear as new angles present themselves. There will be no disagreement between editors that it is the major story, and little discussion about how long it stays the lead. On days when stories are less obvious, the lead may shift around almost from bulletin to bulletin. Indeed, the various news organisations might each choose a different lead. Those are the days when, in newspaper terms, every paper chooses a different story for its banner headline.

Judgements are made on the basis of an international outlook, but bearing national interests in mind. There is continuing debate about the parochial nature of news, and it is not confined to this country. News – anywhere – must have a parochial element because every story must be relevant to the listener. If three people are killed in a boating accident in Rio de Janeiro, how much does the British listener want to know? It will make a difference if all three are from Manchester.

When deciding how to put together a bulletin, an editor must think about the constraints of time and the mixture of items. There may be a 20-second voice report on a story, but only 12 seconds available for it in the bulletin. The story will have to be rewritten to run as copy, read by the newsreader within the time available. Or there may be four copy stories running one after the other, so a cut is moved from another part of the bulletin in order to break the pattern.

A bulletin editor is to news what a producer is to programmes, only bulletins happen every hour. Every 60 minutes the listener's interest must be re-kindled, so every bulletin must be fresh, carry the information the listener should know, and maintain a good mixture of serious news, off-beat and human interest stories. It is no wonder that editors are voracious beasts, forever on the prowl.

CHAPTER 6
Programme production

The role of the producer

Every aspect of a programme is the final responsibility of the producer. Take other people's opinions and ideas into account as much as you like, but in the end your decision as producer must be accepted by everyone else – and if it is wrong, on your head be it. The producer's commitment to the programme differs from that of the other members of the team. Reporters care very much about the items they are responsible for. Presenters care about how the whole programme is put together – after all, they are in the front line when it is on air. But it is the producer who must make all the people and components work well together.

How much planning is long-term and how much short-term is to some extent dictated by the format of a programme. A series or a drama spot can and should be organised well in advance. News and current affairs issues are by definition short-term. How short depends on what it is. If it is a breaking story, be sure it is accurate, but then get it to air fast!

A producer has to have ideas and lots of them. Which ones actually make it must be decided on the basis of the listener finding them interesting or relevant. Even if you are not interested in an item, you decide whether to carry it on the basis of whether people on the top of the bus would be talking about it, or would want to eavesdrop on someone else talking about it. Keep your ears and eyes open – if public transport problems made it difficult for you to get to work, that means the listener also had trouble and will expect you to explain why. Develop at least a curiosity about everything. You may not be interested in sport, or the financial report, or whatever, but the listener is or those spots would not be in the programme.

You must also be well enough informed to be able to decide when an item should stop being run in its specialised spot and start running as general news. Is the winner of the Football Premiership a foregone conclusion, or is it neck and neck, making it worth interviews with the two managers? No subject is boring, but the way it is presented can be.

The producer does not only decide which stories to cover, but also how to present them and how much weight and time to give to each. When reporters are asked to cover a story, the two questions they ask are 'What angle do you want?' and 'How long should it be?' You can think on your feet to some extent, but you should already have an idea of the story's 'weight' (i.e. is it likely to be a lead or a light piece later in the programme) and how much time you think it deserves. Don't be dictatorial. Take the advice of the reporter when the story gets back. It may have turned out to be a cracker, which means you should give the reporter time to dress it up, or it may have ended up dull, in which case drop it and do not waste any more of the reporter's time.

You have a stream of choices as to how to present stories: bring the guest in live during the programme, send a reporter out to do the interview (although even in large stations reporters are a scarce breed), package the item, record a Q & A, etc. If you are producing a phone-in, do you want an expert (e.g. an academic), a pundit (e.g. a journalist who specialises in the subject), or someone with experience of the subject? Which form you opt for depends on the sort of item it is, the programme's format and style, what else is likely to come in, and whether the person you want is free at the necessary or ideal times.

Start out aiming for the ideal, but always stay practical. A great idea may surface, but can your resources stretch far enough to do it justice? Does the idea need to be tailored a bit so it can be done in time? Is it the sort of item you would be better off briefing an outsider to do in order to present you with a finished package?

Always remember you are a communicator; talk to people about what you're thinking and planning and how you expect them to fit in. Get yourself as familiar with any subject as time will allow and then talk to contributors about which areas you are going to cover on air and, sometimes, in what order. A knowledge of at least the basic facts is essential; you cannot speak confidently or authoritatively without it.

You are working with people, so get to know them and their interests. Take in their strengths and weaknesses and use that knowledge in a sensitive but practical way. If, for instance, you know that the guy in forward planning is a railway enthusiast, or a financial reporter goes parachuting at weekends, you could ask their advice about whether a story deserves coverage.

Radio is a flexible medium. In the course of every item you put to air, think about ways of brightening it up and making it lively and memorable. Whenever possible, think in terms of an outside broadcast (OB). If sound effects bring the item closer, use them. One note of caution, though. Never use any sound effect gratuitously. Sounds should be an integral part of an item; do not just throw in a bit of music as a pick-me-up for a programme you think is boring. You have so many choices; never settle for the easy option.

The Radio Authority has become less strict about the separation of editorial material and ads but the distinction between them must not be blurred and must not confuse the listener. We do not have to use a sting between an ad sequence and the programme, unless the ads have a style and format similar to editorial, so stings should also be used positively and in a way the listener has come to expect. If your station generally uses stings as an introduction to something, such as news or sports bulletins, do not start throwing them into your programme willy nilly. The presenter should usually be able to separate ads from the programme, but there are occasions when a sting might be appropriate, such as when an ad warning how not to get AIDS is scheduled in a light programme. Even then, think about it in advance, discuss it with your presenter, and try to find a formula that does not prevent the programme being heard as an integrated whole.

Remember that your programme is just part of the station's output: it is not an island, isolated from the rest. So do not end your programme by making it sound as though the station is signing off air (unless it is). Encourage the listener to stay listening to the programme that follows yours. At some point in the programme – half way through, perhaps, trail your next programme. At the end of the programme, throw ahead to what is coming next.

Programme preparation

You have decided what you are doing and probably where most of the items will fit in. Do your final running order in good time, but not until you are pretty sure that things will not change. If you are using a rough running order as a planner coming up to a programme, photocopy the blank after you have entered ads and out-times (see below). The location of the ads and the length of the breaks make a big difference to your timing. The RA no longer limits the number of ads that can be played each hour; that is now the responsibility of each station.

A running order should be detailed enough for any first-timer, whether producer, presenter, or engineer, to be able to walk in and do the programme. Two examples of running orders are shown here – Classic FM and Talk Radio (Figures 6.1 and 6.2).

Programmes may have different formats, but what each running order has in common is that every sound the listener hears is noted.

Out-times coming up to the top of the hour are when the presenter must stop speaking so that the newsreader can begin exactly on the hour – not a second before or after. There is slightly more flexibility around the out-times for the half-past news summary, but every effort should be made to be as accurate as possible. In either case, the 'hour' is taken for granted, so the times relate to the minutes and seconds.

Each programme will have a fixed format, with the daily variations entered by the producers. There are times, of course, when breaking stories mean the programme as set up has to be scrapped.

It is important that where slugs, durations and out-words appear, they are correct and the same on all related material, i.e. on interviews, tapes, where used, cues and running orders. That is the ideal: there may be circumstances in which it is more important to get the story to air in time than to ensure that all the niceties have been observed. But it is worth making the effort, because consistency in labelling can save mistakes and panics when the programme is going out.

Listen to every item before it goes to air, not only to check for legals, but also to decide placement. It is dangerous to try to judge from the cue alone, because your final judgement can be swayed by anything from the fact that it is a lively tape to the fact that the quality is just not broadcastable. You also need to listen for pots.

Double check out-times both before you get into the studio and within twenty minutes of getting to them once you are inside. If you are working with an engineer, it is helpful to get a second opinion on your maths.

CLASSIC NEWSNIGHT – 18:30 to 19:00 – Thursday 12 June 1998.
Presenter: John Brunning
Editor: Darren Henley

18:29:20 Opening Sequence
[OVER MUSIC BED – THREE HEADLINES – TWO AUDIO CLIPS]

18:30:00 Spending/Fahy   16" CUE + 2'01" PACKAGE
[REPORT BY POL CORR ON CHANCELLOR'S REFORMS OF PUBLIC FINANCES]

18:32:17 Kosovo/Moore   25" CUE + 1'18" INTERVIEW
[INTERVIEW WITH ITN'S DIPLOMATIC EDITOR ROBERT MOORE – ON USE OF NATO FORCES IN KOSOVO]

18:34:00 Cookson/Johnson   15" CUE + 2'41" PACKAGE
[REPORTER OBIT ON LIFE AND WORK OF WRITER CATHERINE COOKSON]

18:36:56 Pill/Blears   16" CUE + 1'56" PACKAGE
[REPORTER PACKAGE ON NEW CAMPAIGN TO MAKE IT EASIER TO GET EMERGENCY CONTRACEPTION]

18:39:08 Asthma/Eykyn   13" CUE + 1'39" PACKAGE
[REPORTER PACKAGE ON POSSIBLE NEW ASTHMA VACCINE]

18:41:00 Weather/Forestier   21" CUE + 2'04" PACKAGE
[REPORTER PACKAGE ON OUR LACK OF SUMMER WEATHER]

18:43:25 Forecast & Trail   60" MUSIC BED WITH WEATHER AND THROW A HEAD TRAIL TO SECOND HALF OF PROG

18:44:25 Commercial Break

18:47:00 Finance News   2'23" PRESENTER READ – INCLUDING 2 AUDIO CLIPS

18:49:23 Sports News   2'07" BULLETIN – READ BY SPORTS PRESENTER

18:51:30 Feature   4'23" INTERVIEW WITH GUITARIST SIMON DINNEGAN MIXED WITH MUSIC FROM NEW CD

18:55:53 Trail   12" TRAIL FOR NEXT DAY'S PROG

18:56:05 Closing Headlines   60" MUSIC BED – MAIN STORIES RE-CAP

18:57:05 Commercial Break

18:59:35 NEXT PROGRAMME [SMOOTH CLASSICS AT SEVEN] BEGINS

Figure 6.1 Although this is the national classical music station, Classic FM does broadcast a nightly Newsnight news programme

SCOTT CHISHOLM
WEDNESDAY 18TH MARCH

9.00 News

Big Issue: After the Budget – is Gordon Brown a family friend or family foe?

9.03
Tape: Robert Snowden, Professor of Family Studies at Exeter University
Dur: 6.04 out 'This is talk radio'

9.10 Ads
Phone: Robert Whelan, assistant director of the Institute of Economic Affairs and author of recent report 'Broken Homes and Battered Children'
Is this a budget for the family – is it a budget for marriage?
Do you think that the government is sending a message that it doesn't matter if a child is raised within a marriage?
What can the government do to encourage the institution of marriage?
Should the government use economics as a form of social engineering?
Isn't it better that any available money goes to children rather than their parents?

9.21 Ads

9.30 Phone: Caerydwyn Roberts, director of the Family Policy Studies Centre
Is this budget good news for the family?
Is Labour re-defining what the family is (i.e. a couple with children, not necessarily married)?
Is this re-definition an attack on the institution of marriage?
Is it good for the family to give mothers incentives to return to work?

9.41 Ads
Phone Lynette Burrows, author of 'Good Children'
Do you think this budget helps the family?
Do you think people are being given the right financial incentives to create the best environment for bringing up children?
Is a family a couple with children, regardless of whether the couple are married?
What else can the government do to shore up the family?

9.47 Ads

9.59 Travel

Figure 6.2 Interview phone-in programmes form a staple diet for independent radio. A good example is the Scott Chisholm programme on Talk Radio

Finally, be sure that all the principals involved in the programme have a copy of the running order, i.e. presenters, engineers, phone-ops, other producers or anyone else who needs to know what is running in the programme and at what time.

Programme preparation check-list

- All items listened through, edited and pot points found.
- Cues checked.
- Running order clearly and fully presented and copied.
- Programme material organised so that it is easy to retrieve.
- Out-times double-checked.
- Be in studio early enough to tidy and equip it, and to test machinery and bring in paper, pens, water and cups.

Studio production

Being a producer is rather like being a chess player, especially in the studio. You have your pieces (the items for air) and a general game plan (the running order), and you have to think at least three moves ahead.

Ideally you should be in the studio at least five minutes before the programme starts to check that the microphones are all working, get a voice level from the presenter, make sure talk-back is all right, and generally ensure that all the machinery is working and ready to use. Give yourself ten minutes if the programme is a phone-in because you will need to check that the phone lines are working. The biggest possible panic on a phone-in is a fault on the on-air switchboard.

Tape: ensure that you have enough ROT tape and take-up spools, labels and some cue paper.

Be sure your presenter is happy, and has everything he or she needs for the programme. Tidy up the studio if necessary, and check that water, cups, paper and pens are available for the presenter and guests. At this stage, the producer is not just a journalist, but a nurse-maid as well. It is the job of a producer to cosset the presenter; the more contented the presenter, the greater the possibility of a good programme. If the preparation for a programme is thorough and well-organised, and everyone working on it starts out contented and confident, then at least you have a chance of getting through it without panics.

Do not allow lax studio discipline. Any non-essential discussion should take place before or after the programme, not over talk-back during an ad or item. It is not unknown for a technical fault to send everything said over talk-back to air. This once happened, and was made worse by the nature of the discussion between the presenter and engineer. Everything that is ever said in front of a mike should be treated as though that mike was 'live' (i.e. switched on).

Before putting any item to air, listen to the first few words in 'play' mode to ensure:

- it is the right item
- the cue fits
- the technical options are right (**tape:** make sure the speed is correct, ½ track, etc.).

Before you put a live guest in the studio, run a final check that you have all the details right (name, title, etc.) and that your presenter/engineer knows what the stand-by item is. You should also have a stand-by ready whenever an item is live. A phone-line or circuit can go down without notice.

Carts: fast cue them to ensure they are properly re-cued. If there is time, play them through at normal speed.

Keep studio engineers informed by giving them copies of cues, preferably in playing order. It is good practice to tell both presenter and engineer the next item, even if it is written on the running order. Always remember, though, that the end of a scripted cue is only a guide; presenters often change scripts without warning. The item should be sent to air only when the presenter has given you a hand cue.

Tape: Make a note at the top of each cue showing which tape machine that item is on. This should prevent the wrong tape going to air. Think three moves ahead. For example, the tape on machine 1 is going out, the one on 2 is checked and lined up for air, and now there is time to mosey out to the newsroom and collect the headlines for the half-past summary, if read by the presenter. Before you leave the control room, be sure both the engineer and the presenter know that the next item is ready. This ensures the smoothest possible gear-change if something goes wrong. If an edit breaks on tape 1, for example, the presenter can apologise and move on without panic to the next item even if the producer is not in the control room to give the instruction. Never leave the presenter abandoned and groping for words because you have not thought far enough ahead.

If there are changes to the running order during the programme (and there often are), tell the presenter on talk-back, then back it up on the screen if you have that facility and leave it there until that sequence is finished and you are back to programme as scheduled. If the control room does not have a screen, confirm what the next item is going to be with the presenter until the programme gets back on course. Change both your running order, for the sake of the P as B (see below) as well as keeping it straight, and the engineer's. Remember you are a communicator: tell all the appropriate people what is happening.

If a big story breaks, the newsdesk or reporter should tell the producer, the producer then tells the presenter and engineer how coverage will be handled. The producer must always be in charge, which means being alert, ahead of the game, informed and confident.

On the cover of *The Hitch-hiker's Guide to the Galaxy* was that 'helpful' instruction, 'DON'T PANIC', which is the producer's golden rule in the studio. If the producer panics, everyone else has no option but to panic as well. Presenters are responsible for making programmes sound smooth and giving the impression that everything is under control. That may not be possible if the production team leaves them in the lurch.

After the programme, tidy up the control room and the studio.

Tape: check that there are take-up spools on the tape machines and some ROT tape available, and that the studio area is in the state you would like to find it when you arrive.

Finally, sit down and fill out the P as B. This stands for 'Programme as Broadcast' and determines how all the contributors get paid. List everything that went out on the programme, which items need to be paid for, who should be paid and how much. If you used any music in the programme, you must complete a music log so that royalties can be assessed and paid. If you fail to fill out the music log the Performing Rights Society will eventually ban the playing of any music on the station as a whole! No producer likes the paper work, but it is a necessary evil.

The multi-skilled producer

On the way to becoming the programme producer, most journalists will have become proficient in the many, often unexpected, duties of

Programme production 69

phone operator, researcher and assistant producer and have developed studio operational skills to a high degree of competence.

- They will start by greeting guests.
- They will carry out basic research, reading cuttings and listening to previous interviews or speeches.
- They will set up interviews, persuading guests to come to the studio or, secondarily, organising an ISDN or telephone interview.
- They will write cues and questions.
- They will be a telephone operator, a tough and dextrous task in phone-in programmes.
- They will be able to operate all forms of mixers.
- They will be able to use all forms of portable recorders.
- They will be able to programme digital equipment.
- They will be able to edit digitally and cut tape.
- They will drive the desk in transmission as well as producing the programme and sometimes carrying out the duty of sequence editor.

Presenters

If journalists resist the temptation of moving into management, they may aspire to become presenters – the most onerous yet most rewarding radio job. They are the voices of the station, the people listeners relate to and identify with.

The role of presenter has become even more intense and complicated with the almost universal use of self-operation. Probably the most complex of all operations in the network is that of the newsreader in News Direct 97.3, London's rolling news station, now broadcasting in a 20:20:20 format. Figure 6.3 shows presenter Jonathan Staples preparing to read the news; in front of him are eight television screens and four keyboards. If presenters can cope with operations of this complexity, they can handle any operation.

Programme formats

All programmes must have a format. Because stations break down into departments (programmes, newsroom, sport, etc.), we each have a tendency to concentrate on the area we are involved in, but the listener does not. Most of the people who listen to the radio never think about the components involved in what they hear. They hear

70 A Guide to Commercial Radio Journalism

Figure 6.3 The eight screens are: *top row, from left,* TV, ITN raw feeds, TV ring main (e.g. House of Commons, sport), video link with newsroom; *bottom row, from left,* AA touchscreen, DAVE-2 for audio, DAVE-1 playlist, DCS for ads, jingles, promos. There are five keyboards; two for DAVEs, one for DCS, one for the Hot Keys and one for the router/switcher. The presenter is wearing a headset microphone because he will continually move his head to look at screens. There is also a guest microphone for interviews (photos: John Greenwood)

the station as a whole, and so must you. That includes ads, headlines, fixed spots (which should not be cued as if they were boring time fillers), city and sports reports, etc. Integrate them into the programme. All these ingredients are there for positive reasons. You may not be interested, but the listener is.

Time of day is an important consideration in deciding type of programme and format. Early-morning listeners are probably either getting ready for work or travelling to work. Studies indicate that they want, in roughly this order of preference, news, weather, travel information, sport, and time checks. Programmes have to serve up these ingredients regularly, because each listener may tune in for only 30 or 40 minutes, with interruptions for brushing teeth, boiling the kettle, etc. The format of the programme may act as a back-up, or even replacement, for the clock: a commuter may know that by the time a particular sports report begins, he or she should be leaving to catch the train.

By the time 9 or 10 o'clock rolls round, the listener is assumed to be able to give longer spans of attention, so programmes that require more listener involvement can be scheduled. And so on through the day.

Magazine programmes and phone-ins are the two most common formats used in all-talk broadcasting. But there are other formats which can be programmes in their own right, or be mixed together in some form:

- **Discussion programmes**: a number of participants sit 'round the table' to air different views on an issue, with the presenter as the arbiter or chairman of the discussion.
- **Commentaries**: reporters or presenters describe an event, e.g. a football match, or the ceremony on Remembrance Sunday.
- **Drama**: this can be anything from a clever ad to a dramatic reading.
- **Features**: extended personal item with more than one interviewee and using sound effects and music.
- **Documentaries**: an extended investigation of an issue, with several interviewees and sound effects.

Each requires a different approach, but all need a format so that everyone participating in the programme knows where they are at all times – including the listener.

Generally, taking an interview from one programme and dropping it into another does not always work, even if the subject matter is similar. For instance, if a news magazine programme did an interview with a Health Minister, what that person said in the interview may be relevant to a phone-in programme about health issues, but it might sound odd actually to play it. That is because the presentation styles would be very different, the pace of the two programmes would not be the same, and the formats themselves require different levels of involvement from the listener. These three elements are the basics of any format. But the Health Minister may say something that can be used as a news cut and also form the basis of a wrap. What the Health Minister said can, of course, be paraphrased and used in the phone-in.

Presentation style

This is the most important feature of any programme because it establishes consistency and distinguishes the sound of a station. With so many stations available, it is essential to create a station 'sound', so that it is easily identifiable in the spectrum cacophony. The listener gets to know and trust a particular style. Whether a programme maintains and, more important, builds audience figures often depends on whether listeners will accept a specific personality in their homes. They invite you in but can throw you out simply by turning a switch.

It is the job of the programme team to make the presentation style work to its best advantage. That does not mean giving in to a presenter's limitations or allowing the programme to be distorted. It means knowing what material the presenter is naturally comfortable with and when you need to tailor, research or talk through items.

Some people argue that a presenter should write, or re-write, all cues and links so as to maintain an individual style. Whether this is possible depends on the type of programme, the time of day and the presenter. If you end up composing a programme script that someone else is going to read, write it to suit the reader, not to suit you.

Pace

Pace is dictated by both presentation style and the level of listener involvement. A breakfast-time news programme, for example, has a crisp approach and expects the listener to be able to make sharp mental changes of direction, whereas an hour-long phone-in on a single issue expects the listener to concentrate on details. Within a general format pace can be varied for effect, time constraints, or availability of material. Just be aware of what the standard pace is and why you are changing it.

Listener involvement

How much involvement you can demand depends on what the listener is likely to be doing. It would be unreasonable to expect the same level of attention from someone trying to get a family organised and off to school or work as from that same person doing the ironing. The golden rule, however, is one that has been mentioned before: always treat the listener as an individual. Do not present your programme to a mass audience, but to one, singular, person.

Magazine programmes

Magazine programmes do not simply consist of a series of individual items, even if the running order makes it look that way. They are integrated programmes made up of linked components. In the same way as you need to 'hear' a cue as you write it, you need to 'hear' a programme as it is set out on a running order. Don't put an item about someone dying of cancer next to a jokey piece. Stories involving death should be run only among other serious stories, and if a death story or serious story is the last in a sequence, pay attention to what sort of ad will follow it. If you are forced to put unsuitable items next to or near each other, the programme team should discuss how to deal with the problem so that the presenter can cope once the programme is on air. Again, check that there are no unsuitable ads nearby.

The presenter of a magazine programme needs to integrate the components to keep the programme flowing as a whole. Items should not be treated as though they had dropped in from another planet, but reacted to in the same way as a live interview. If, for instance, there is a light-hearted piece going out on air, and the presenter back-announces it in a dry, straightforward manner, that will have a jarring effect on the listener. The tone used by the presenter should suit that of the item.

A bit of thought as to placement and perhaps the addition of a phrase to the top of a cue can work wonders in terms of integrating items in a programme. Say you are kicking off a programme hour with a report from Washington on President Clinton's difficulties in getting Congress to approve his candidate for appointment as Attorney General followed by a report about the latest problems President Yeltsin is having with the Duma to approve his choice of Prime Minister. On paper, you might start out without any scripted back-anno for the Washington piece, and the start of the Moscow cue might be: 'In Moscow, Boris Yeltsin is being frustrated with another challenge to his plans for a new government.' If you now insert at the top of the Moscow cue: 'Stephen Bonden reporting from Washington. And while President Clinton is at odds with his Congress, the Russian president is having to deal with problems of his own,' you will have achieved two ends. The Washington item has been back-announced, and a bridge has been formed to the next item.

Be careful not to misuse or overdo these sorts of links. If a story is completely unrelated to the previous item, tell the listener so by using the right words and voice inflection. You need to take the listener with you from item to item. Signpost changes of direction, and try to keep the sequence as logical as possible.

When you are cueing up live interviews, you must have some idea of what each answer will be in order to keep it logical. Sometimes the only way to achieve this is by having a 'pre-interview interview' on the phone. Contributors tend to appreciate such chats because it gives them some idea of the areas you want to cover.

The programme should be organised flexibly so that the format works for you rather than you slaving away to it. Do not let the format force you to run certain items at certain times. To return to the example of the pieces from Moscow and Washington, you might have decided to run Washington as your lead at the top of the hour, and then use the Moscow one as the lead after the headlines at half past the hour. Many news magazines use the second lead at the half hour in order to spread the interest and weight through the hour.

Each programme should, in a sense, emulate something like a spinach and bacon salad. The spinach is tasty but soft, and every now and then you come across a bit of crisp, salty bacon. Every item in the programme should be able to stand on its own in terms of relevance and interest, but the listener should not be bombarded with a sequence of items that are all too similar in subject or style of presentation. Try to achieve an interesting mixture of Q & As, wraps, live interviews, etc., that still allow the programme to flow.

You should have time in the planning stage of the programme to make a cool calculation of what sort of news day it is going to be. If it is a bad one, you will end up going for stories that you would normally never consider. If a big story is breaking, it will dominate the programme and other news will need to be edited down to fit into whatever crevices are left. Make life easier for yourself by doing as much as possible as early as possible. That way, if a story breaks just before the programme goes to air you will be able to concentrate on it rather than on the material you could have processed an hour before.

Initiate more stories than you have space for. There are two reasons for doing this. First, there will always be some stories that do not materialise for one reason or another. Secondly, as a former editor of ITN put it, any programme is only as good as what has been left out. So if your programme usually requires a dozen items to fill it, initiate at least fifteen. Be aware of what reporters and specialists, where available, are doing and put them on stand-by for a last minute appearance to save the day.

Magazine programmes tend to present a slice of life. Each programme should reflect a healthy personality, with a good general mixture of serious and light items, art, sport, money interests, etc. The listener may not be an expert in every field, but will probably be an armchair aficionado in at least one, and interested in them all.

Phone-ins

Phone-ins play a major role in all radio stations and are one of the strengths of commercial radio in particular. Letters to the station are fine up to a point but they have to be read out and lack the spontaneity and surprise of a live call. OK, they may be considered cheap to produce but they are not that cheap. But they do have the attraction of letting people talk. At one stage, it was difficult to persuade listeners to talk but that is increasingly no longer the case. Perhaps we are becoming more like Americans who are so voluble and are so willing to give their views. Over the years, callers have come to understand the procedure and what is expected of them. They have learnt to be callers.

Phone-ins may seem easier to put together than magazines. Only one item has to be set up, and the callers do a lot of the hard work by deciding what questions to put. Unfortunately, however, phone-ins can be much more stressful. For a start, you do not have the cushion of setting up more items than you need. Finding the right person, who is free to discuss the subject at the right time, can be a nightmare. The choice of guest is crucial. You have to take care with the timing of subjects for discussion. People can only comment in retrospect. Ask for thoughts on what is going to happen tomorrow and few calls result; but try again the day after an event has taken place and callers have had time to be made aware of the issue and to have thought about it. You are also dependent on the callers' active involvement. It is difficult to have a good phone-in when no one rings up.

The initial interview with a guest is different, too. It is an interview with holes, that is, the presenter does not pursue a line of questioning to the limit but leaves gaps, hoping that callers will fill them in. If this does not happen, the interviewer can always say: ' I'd like to go back and ask you more about ...'.

Phone-ins are so flexible. You can start with calls on the main issue of the day, triggered by an interview – with Gordon Brown on the Budget, for example. Bring in the shadow spokesperson to challenge the Budget (shadows are often more available than ministers). Move on to an interview with a film star, a singer, a writer. Listeners love to say that they have talked to Jack Nicholson or Harrison Ford or Brad Pitt or Joseph Heller or Maya Angelou or Kate Winslett. Ideas and opinions of stars are usually not as important for the phone-in. Stars have presence. Writers usually have more to say. Invite statesmen, thinkers, critics onto the programme. Again, this gives callers the opportunity to question Tony Blair, William Hague, Harriet Harman, Lady Thatcher, Lord Callaghan, Stephen Gould, Archbishop Tutu.

Give advice. The world is full of people wanting advice and comfort – about relationships, health, bringing up children, finance. Phone-ins fulfil a need.

Go to general calls. If the calls are on one topic, take lots, quickly, to create interest through pace, if not content. Ask callers to speak for one minute only on a topic of their choice, without interruption.

Invite guests to talk on an issue of their choice, preferably controversial but certainly interesting, and defend it for, say, half an hour against callers.

Initiate and incorporate a phone vote on an issue. The result is not as balanced and as representative as a properly conducted opinion poll, but it is an indication of the views of many of the people listening to the station.

On great events, they do give an impression of what people are feeling – the death of Princess Diana, and before that, the daily calls during the wars in the Gulf and the Falklands. Oral historians have found they are a useful and fascinating source.

As to the subjects, which ones spark interest is always a wonder. How the police carry out their duty, for example, is an important issue which affects people's lives, but the subject seldom provokes a lively response. But mention arthritis, and the switchboard lights up.

Phone-ins are a little slice of democracy, letting the listener finally have a say on the issues of the day, or even complain about an aspect of the station's output. They are a form of active radio, in which listeners take part rather than the more usual passive radio provided by radio stations. That's fine, but the listener's contribution must come from an acceptable source.

Calls from pay phones should not be allowed on air because call boxes are largely for people to use in an emergency. A contributor to a phone-in could tie up a call box for ten minutes or more. There is no way of checking whether a pay phone is in someone's house, so it is a blanket ban. It can be difficult to recognise instantly whether a call emanates from a phone box, but use your ears and try to establish that the call is from a personal phone.

It is against the law to drive and speak into a hand-held mobile phone. You must be sure that the caller has pulled over and stopped before taking the call. And that means they have to stop legally. A caller's contribution was once halted prematurely because he had stopped on the hard shoulder of a motorway: he had to stop speaking to the programme and start speaking to the policeman.

There are also technical reasons for being tough on callers from both pay phones and car phones. Calls from phone boxes inevitably go to air just as the pips sound and the money runs out. Car phones offer what can only be called 'variable' line quality so even if the caller is a passenger, do not take the call until they have pulled over. The sound of the programme comes first, and keeping a phone-in on course and interesting is hard enough without inviting problems.

Five questions must be answered positively before taking any call:

- Is the line broadcastable? No matter how good a point is, if it is inaudible it is a non-point. Ask the caller to ring back, or take the number and ring back. If it is an interesting point, keep trying until you get a decent line.
- Is the caller coherent? If the person is inarticulate to the point of being unable to make a clear point, the pace of the programme will be destroyed while the presenter tries to hack through the morass. People who are a bit tipsy are dangerous, so keep the contribution short and your finger over the prof button. Those who have had so much to drink as to put them into the inarticulate category should not be inflicted on the sober listener.
- Is the point relevant? People's ideas of what areas are associated with any subject never cease to amaze. Someone must keep them to the point, and it is better if that person is the producer rather than the presenter. If the programme is taking general callers, spe-

cialised questions should not get through: a presenter is not a specialist.
- Is there sufficient time to deal with the point? It is frustrating if there is less than a minute left before the programme ends and an interesting point needing two minutes has to be cut short. Better to take details of the call and start a subsequent programme with it.
- Is the caller able to hang on until the presenter is ready? Unlike the BBC, we do not call back every contributor, and it can cause bedlam in the control room and possible confusion on air if a caller hangs up just as the presenter gets to that line. But if you know that a caller is likely to have to wait for ten minutes or more before actually getting to air, it is only fair to ring him or her back. You don't want to put people off ringing in because their phone bills are rocketing.

Life is made much easier if your station has screens that link the control room with the presenter. Details of who has called, what about and in what order calls should be taken can be 'stacked' on the screen. Regardless of how the control room communicates with the studio, however, before any details go up on the screen or its equivalent you must ensure the following:

- There is a clear understanding of what the caller wants to say.
- All the details have been entered on the phone log, i.e. the caller's name, the area he or she is calling from (if relevant), the topic to be discussed, and the caller's telephone number. Without the first and last of those, you are in breach of RA guidance.
- The caller's radio is either off or far enough away not to be heard. Callers get desperately confused if they can hear the radio. The programme is going out in delay, so they hear themselves up to ten seconds after they have actually spoken, and callers inevitably listen to the radio rather than the phone.
- The caller agrees to hold on unless you agree that you will phone back.
- The caller is properly switched through to air and standing by.

These steps are usually short-circuited when there is a shortage of calls, although that is exactly when they ought to be strictly adhered to. If the presenter has been filling air time, waiting longer than usual for someone to call, it is understandable that the caller may get on air before all the details are in front of the presenter.

Telephone log sheets should at least contain the caller's name, telephone number and which line they have phoned in on. The RA says the logs should be kept 'for a time' in case there is a need to get back to someone, whether for legal or other reasons. Phone logs are always confidential unless the programme format makes it obvious to callers that their number will be made available to other callers.

Phone operators

Phone-ops should be briefed carefully. They are your first line of defence, so be sure they know what sort of calls you are willing to take on any programme or subject. They have to be sharp. They have to understand quickly the point being made by the caller; they have to assess its relevance to the programme topic; they have to advise the producer; they have to be diplomatic. Phone-ops have arguably the worst job in a radio station. It is hard enough for them to deal with the callers; don't make the job worse by being vague.

General open line

You need to give the listeners some idea of the range of subjects you would like to cover at the start of the programme, and also indicate whether they will be allowed to introduce subjects. Consider the parameters you would apply in ideal circumstances, but if the calls are slow, shelve the ideal world and broaden your horizons. If calls are not the most exciting, generate interest by taking calls quickly. Interest can be created by pace. There are times when a caller will introduce a subject out of the blue that will virtually take over the programme. Just hope that the subject is interesting and fun, and not yet another discussion on an issue that has already been talked to death; and it has to be a particularly dull day for either dog licences or pensions to be inspiring subjects.

The producer and presenter should have discussed enough possible ideas and angles for callers to consider so that the presenter is not left floundering. Organising the format so there is a break between the introductory remarks and taking the first call creates a bit more time for the listener to get through.

As in all other types of programme, but especially phone-ins because they are continuously live, producers should never leave presenters in the dark. Let the presenter know if the phone panel is busy but full of cranks, or if calls are slow, or they are all labouring a point that has already been made. The presenter is in a position to do something positive about the problem: 'I think we've pretty much dealt with the death of Princess Diana for the time being, but I'd be interested in what you think about this morning's assassination of the American President.'

Develop an antenna that is always up. Non-broadcasters are going to air and there is just no telling what they might come out with. You need to have a sixth sense that warns you when someone is straying into a dangerous area. The tone of a caller often gives an indication that the call might become unsuitable.

Specific subject with guest

Remember the listener: does anybody care about the issue? If so, is it a topic people will have something to say about?

Any 'expert' you have not heard on air before should be taken through a thorough pre-booking chat about the area you want to cover. Be sure you have the right person who can talk well. Be sure that person is capable of fielding a wide range of questions. Don't commit yourself when you first contact a possible guest. Say something along these lines: 'We're thinking about doing a programme on ———, and I wondered if I could ask you a few questions about it.' You can then have a conversation about the subject, and if your expert turns out not to be satisfactory, you can gracefully exit.

Explain to every guest that it is a phone-in and how callers get to air (i.e. what sort of screening process takes place). If the subject you want to discuss has more than one side to it (and most do), decide whether to have other sides represented or do a follow-up programme later. Set up the various sides before airing one, and tell all guests what you are doing.

Be careful about setting up consumer specialities. Such programmes often create a lot of listener interest, which is the point of the exercise, but can lead to a string of complaints too specific for any other listener to relate to. Besides, the advice tends to be much the same for everybody.

Profanity (called 'prof' or 'Dump')

The red button is used more for libel and contempt than for four-letter words. It is fair enough for someone to complain about the standards of consumer items, say, but not specifically a particular pen company being in cahoots with a clothing-maker because their pens inevitably leak in your inside pocket (which Spike Milligan once did during a live interview when we were not in prof).

If a dodgy comment slips through the net, get rid of the offending call and distance the station from the statement ('Come on, millions have chosen that product. I'm sure if you have a particular complaint, you'll write to the company. We'll leave you to get on with your letter while we talk to ...')

Biro, Kleenex and Hoover are generic terms for ball-point pens, paper tissues and vacuum cleaners, but that does not save you from libel. If a company or brand name is used you are on dangerous ground.

CHAPTER 7
Responsibilities, objectivity and confidentiality

Reporting events, whether local or international, is one of the most important services any radio station provides. Even if the main format of a station is music-based, people depend on the radio to tell them what is happening when a major story breaks. Its flexibility and immediacy make radio the perfect medium for fast-breaking news. This is a big advantage, but it is also a responsibility. It is a responsibility which, quite rightly, is mainly carried by us – the broadcasters. The government can stop particular programmes, and this country does have more legal constraints than most, but we still do operate a so-called 'free press'. The government does not tell us what to report or how, so it is up to us to be sure that we deserve the listener's confidence.

Lord Donaldson, giving his judgment in the Spycatcher Appeal in February 1988, gave a pretty good definition of journalism: '... the media are the eyes and ears of the general public. They act on behalf of the general public. Their right to know and their right to publish is neither more nor less than that of the general public. Indeed it is that of the general public for whom they are trustees.' The relevant point here is that while journalists have to be vigilant on behalf of the public, they do not have any special rights enshrined in law to carry out that vigilance.

What is news?

News = new, interesting, true.

The paraphrase of Robert McLeish's definition of news captures the essence of what news stories must contain and convey. News must also be informative and relevant. A story may be interesting, but does it matter to the listener? Even if a story is complicated and difficult to explain in a few sentences, it is your job to find the right words and make the story relevant to your listener.

Every item you send to air must get all the facts right, because the listener is depending on you and has no way of checking on what you have said. If it turns out that what you have reported is wrong in any way, the listener will not believe anything else you report later on. That loss of trust affects not just you but the entire station, so be sure to get all the details right, including names, initials, titles and figures.

Speaking of figures, remember the old dictum that they can be made to say anything: make their meaning clear. Be especially careful with percentages, which must be put in context. A large percentage increase in crime in a given area is meaningless if the boundaries of that area have changed since the last figures were compiled.

If at any time you are not sure of a fact, the rule is return to source. If you are writing up some information for use on air and realise you have not made a complete note of the details you need to include, pick up the phone and find out. If that is not possible, you should attribute or qualify the facts in the story.

If for some reason that is not possible, the other golden rule is if in doubt, leave it out. This is a phrase you will often hear in newsrooms because it is basic to the job. Part of a journalist's responsibilities is to get across new and important information, but if for any reason you are not absolutely sure that something is right, it's better not to run it at all.

There are a lot of golden rules in radio and in journalism, but 'return to source' and 'if in doubt, leave it out' are particularly important because if you adhere to them you will never lie to the listener.

Objectivity

MPs like Tony Benn has been known to point out to interviewers that he was elected, while they were not. Even if the interviewer is asking a question the elector might well have put had it been possible, Mr Benn has a point. The listener has selected you, not elected you. Those who take decisions over our lives have been elected on the basis of their opinions and promises. You don't take those sorts of decisions, and your opinions are irrelevant.

That you think carefully about what you do is obviously important, but your job is to present facts and other people's opinions in an objective way so that the listener can make up his or her own mind. Objectivity is an important concept in journalism but difficult to achieve in practice. To be truly objective we would need to divorce ourselves from our backgrounds and prejudices. There is a long-standing debate about whether this is possible, but you should at least know your own prejudices and confine them to a part of your mind that becomes inoperative when you are doing your job. You will find it easier to interview people who do not hold the same views as you do, simply because you will be able to think of the opposing arguments more quickly. Remember that it is always your job to find the opposite point of view and put it. There are very few one-sided issues. If for some reason you are forced to give only one side of a story, you owe it to the listener to explain why.

There are problematic areas, of course. For instance, is that person carrying a gun a 'terrorist' or a 'freedom fighter'? Often the solution is to use only strictly accurate terms. The general rule is to reflect what is considered the view of the majority of the country. If violent acts occur in your country, they will be seen as acts of terrorism, unless war has been declared. If they take place in foreign dictatorships, they are often described as the work of freedom fighters.

But there are times when objectivity is not possible. In the reporting of events in Northern Ireland, in order to 'starve the terrorist of the oxygen of publicity', the Home Secretary banned broadcasters using any statement made by anyone sympathetic to the aims of certain prescribed organisations, even if that person was an elected councillor representing one of those organisations. This made it very difficult to present objective reports.

It is important to present facts and opinions so that the listener can form a fair assessment, but there are times when the listener does not expect objectivity. When stories are difficult to report because of their social context, stand back and think about what the listener would consider right and wrong. In coverage of Northern Ireland, it would not be socially acceptable for reports to seem to condone terrorism even if they pass a purely objective test. There were disagreements about the coverage of the shooting of children in Dunblane. Did the media intrude on people's grief? Were the descriptions of what happened in the school too graphic? While some of these questions overlap with those of good taste, they also have to do with objective considerations of how much of the story to tell and how much to leave out.

You will sometimes have to decide whether to report on an issue that the majority of people might well put into the 'wrong' category. Should you use that argument not to give air time to the National Front because their views are racist and an incitement to prejudice, or for the view that they should be given enough rope to hang themselves? (There are laws against incitement to racial hatred, and if you had opted for the second argument, you would have had to lose your objectivity if a discussion began to stray into an area that contravened the law.)

It is generally accepted that democracy works on the basis of society making moral, political and social decisions in an atmosphere of free debate. It is part of our job to present the debate, but from as neutral a standpoint as possible.

Accuracy

The Radio Authority codes oblige radio journalists to ensure that all broadcasts are presented with due accuracy and impartiality. Any mistakes have to be corrected as quickly as possible and an apology broadcast where appropriate. Reconstructions have to be sign-posted. Programming intended to re-examine past events involving trauma, including crime, should take care to minimise the potential distress to surviving victims or surviving relations in re-telling the story. Simulated news broadcasts or news flashes have to be sign-posted to avoid the Orson Welles 'War of the Worlds' panic of 1938.

Confidentiality

Journalists use the phrase 'the right to know' frequently, and quite rightly. This country has more legal restrictions on reporting than almost any other, but within those bounds it is our job to keep important facts and issues in the public arena.

It is a journalist's job to uncover and report on issues that some might prefer did not become public, and it is not unusual for the courts to become involved in the tussle of deciding whether certain stories should be told, and by whom. Traditionally, journalists do not 'reveal their sources', and some reporters and editors have been fined or even jailed for upholding that tradition.

The 1984 Police and Criminal Evidence Act offers journalists some protection for confidentiality with one hand, but takes it away with the other. While part of the Act protects 'journalistic material' and gives reporters the opportunity to argue in court against having to reveal information that has been collected, another section allows police to search for and seize material by applying to a circuit judge for a warrant.

Article 10 of the 1981 Contempt of Court Act states that a court shall not require a person to disclose the source of information which is the basis of a broadcast publication unless the court is satisfied that disclosure is necessary:

- for the prevention of disorder,
- for the prevention of crime,

- in the interest of the administration of justice,
- in the interests of national security.

The first test case concerned the *Guardian* newspaper which had received classified government documents from junior civil servant Sarah Tisdall. The *Guardian* was forced to hand it over because the Court of Appeal threatened sequestration of its economic assets. Sarah Tisdall went to jail for 6 months.

The most spectacular defence on source protection was achieved by the journalist William Goodwin who refused to disclose the source of information about Tetra Ltd. The case meandered through the High Court, Appeal Court and reached the House of Lords where he was fined £5,000 in April 1990. Six years later, the European Court of Human Rights decided that the British courts had breached article 10. The European judges said 'sources could be deterred from assisting the press in informing the public on matters of public interest. As a result the vital public watchdog role of the press could be undermined and the ability of the press to provide accurate and reliable information could be adversely affected.'

Generally the law of confidentiality, as it is broadly known, is used not to protect or help journalists, but to stop them publishing particular kinds of information. Thus the courts will protect facts that have been obtained by someone in confidential circumstances. This has traditionally been used to stop employees or former employees from divulging a company's secrets.

The law has been extended, however, notably in the Spycatcher case in which the courts agreed with the government's argument that Peter Wright, along with all former security service employees, had a life-long duty of confidentiality. The Australian courts did not agree, so, even though the government fought to prevent it, publication of *Spycatcher* went ahead there. There was no attempt to prevent publication in the US, possibly because of the provisions of the Constitution. This duty of confidentiality has now been written into the Official Secrets Act.

Good taste

News is often 'bad news', and journalists often end up reporting the unsavoury side of life. This is where considerations of 'good taste' come in.

Stories that involve disasters can cause a lot of distress to the listener. If there has been an earthquake or a plane crash involving large numbers of people, we all have a moment's fear, wondering whether anyone we know is involved. You can reduce some of the distress by giving as much information as you can as soon as you can.

When the Swansea–Paddington rail crash story first broke, anyone who knew someone who was, or might have been, travelling by rail at about the time of the crash would have been worried about them. When details of which trains were involved started coming in, where they had been travelling from, and so on, at least some listeners' fears could be put to rest. Ask yourself what questions the listener is asking, then answer them early on in the report. This is not just good taste, it is also good journalism.

Be conscious of the dangers of causing offence. Sex, race and religion are supposed to be taboo subjects at dinner parties, because someone is bound to offend someone else. They cannot be taboo on the air, but think about how and why you are describing someone. Not all black people are immigrants, not all Jewish people are Zionists. And in either case, is the label relevant to the story?

If the story involves sex, don't be salacious or squalid. Choose your words as if you were at that dinner party, talking to people you do not know very well and do not want to offend. Use proper or medical terms when you can, remembering that the listener will need to understand them.

You will be accused of bad taste if you place inappropriate items next to one another. To use an extreme example, do not follow the Swansea–Paddington rail crash story with one about new excursion fares for holiday-makers. The listener's sensibilities will be bruised. Be aware of which ads are running. Most stations operate a policy of pulling related ads off air if there is a major story running. It is simply bad taste to report the horrors of a major air crash and follow it with a chirpy jingle extolling the virtues of an airline. The advertisers not only understand this policy, they encourage it. The ads can be re-scheduled to run later when they will not be offensive.

Portrayal of violence

The Radio Authority says that violence must never be glorified, and the degree of violence portrayed or described must be essential to the integrity of the item. This rule is relevant to the reporting of sexual crimes and rape trials. Radio is regarded as an intimate medium of communication, so explicit description can have a greater impact on the imagination and be more upsetting for emotionally insecure listeners.

Code on Fairness and Privacy

The Broadcasting Standards Commission published a Code on Fairness and Privacy which became effective from 1 January 1998. The code is more rigorously imposed and onerous than the BBC's 'Producers' Guidelines' because a complaint to the BSC can lead to quasi-legal proceedings and the statutory sanction compels the erring broadcast organisation to publish the BSC's adjudication. The BSC code also has greater detail and presumption of authority over professional standards than the Radio Authority codes.

For example, there is a comprehensive section setting out the protocol for 'dealing fairly with contributors' that imposes at least eight requirements. Interviewees should:

1. be told what the programme is about;
2. be given a clear explanation of why they were contacted by the programme;
3. be told what kind of contribution they are expected to make – for example by way of interview or as part of a discussion;
4. be informed about the areas of questioning, and, wherever possible, the nature of other likely contributions;
5. be told whether their contribution is to be live or recorded, and, if recorded, whether it is likely to be edited;
6. not be coached or pushed or improperly induced into saying anything which they know not to be true or do not believe to be true;
7. whenever appropriate, be made aware of any significant changes to the programme as it develops which might reasonably affect their original consent to participate, and cause material unfairness; and
8. if offered an opportunity to preview the programme, be given clear information about whether they will be able to effect any change in the programme.

News journalism

The BSC qualifies this code of news journalism. It says: 'the speed of news gathering means that it is not always possible to provide contributors to news reports with all the information mentioned above. However, that does not absolve journalists from treating contributors fairly or ensuring that the reports compiled meet the needs of fairness and accuracy.'

Phone-ins

The BSC has a specific directive on accuracy which warns that 'broadcasters should also be alert to the danger of unsubstantiated allegations being made by participants to live phone-ins and discussion programmes and ensure that presenters are briefed accordingly'.

Balance

Its code also sets up an obligation to 'balance' so that 'where a programme alleges wrong-doing or incompetence, or contains a damaging critique of an individual or organisation, those criticised should normally be given an appropriate and timely opportunity to respond to or comment on the arguments and evidence contained within that programme'.

Obtaining material

Any infringement of privacy has to be justified by an overriding public interest in disclosure of the information. Moreover, the means of obtaining the information must be proportionate to the matter under investigation. Privacy can be infringed during the obtaining of material for a programme, even if none of it is broadcast, as well as in the way in which material is used within the programme.

Private and public lives

For much of the time, the private lives of most people are of no legitimate public interest, but when people are caught up, however involuntarily, in events which have a place in the news, their situation should not be abused or exploited.

People in the public eye, their immediate family and their friends do not forfeit the right to privacy, though there may be occasions where private behaviour raises broader public issues either through the nature of the behaviour itself or by the consequences of it becoming widely known. The location of a person's home or family should not normally be revealed unless strictly relevant to the behaviour under investigation.

Recordings

Radio journalists must be sure that words and actions by people are sufficiently in the public domain to justify their broadcast without express permission being sought. Telephone interviewees and participants must have given consent to the use of their contributions prior to broadcast and telephone conversations may not be broadcast without the permission of the participants except in the rare cases where there is an investigation of allegedly criminal or otherwise disreputable behaviour.

Approval at senior management level in the station has to be given for clandestine recording for broadcast of telephone interviews.

Hidden microphones and eavesdropping

The use of hidden microphones to record or broadcast the words of people who are unaware that they are being recorded or broadcast is only acceptable when it is clear that the material acquired is essential to establish the credibility and authority of the story and where the story itself is equally clearly of important public interest.

Radio journalists are not permitted to use information obtained by listening into emergency service radio frequencies. Under Section 5 of the Wireless Telegraphy Act 1949, obtaining information about any radio message which the listener is not authorised to receive is an offence and so is passing on information about an intercepted message, whoever did the intercepting. Therefore the notorious 'Squidgy' tape featuring the private conversation between the late Diana, Princess of Wales and James Hewitt, and the 'Camillagate' tape featuring the private conversation between Prince Charles and Camilla Parker Bowles could not be broadcast on United Kingdom independent radio under any circumstances.

Other areas of responsibility

Protecting young listeners

The Radio Authority expects radio journalists to show sensitivity in the content and style of bulletins when young people under the age of 18 are listening. In particular care should be taken with pre-teenage audiences with respect to strong language, explicit news reports or programming which covers explicitly violent or sexual topics.

Language

Bad language can only be defended in terms of context and authenticity. There is more understanding over the use of offensive language in news and documentary programmes, but the Radio Authority is utterly against bad language and blasphemy in programmes aimed at young listeners or when audience research indicates they might be expected to be listening in significant numbers. Strong language is often used in public order situations and radio reporters should consider further approval before including it in news bulletins.

Medical and alternative medical subjects

Care has to be taken when covering stories about controversial or novel forms of treatment and when claims are made for particular healing powers or properties. The Radio Authority states that programmes on medical subjects must obtain competent professional advice and on matters of potential controversy the programme should give a hearing to more than one opinion.

Chequebook journalism

Chequebook journalism and payment to witnesses in criminal trials by independent radio journalists is absolutely forbidden.

- No payment is to be made to a criminal whose sentence has not yet been discharged.
- No payment is to be made to former criminals for interviews about their crimes.
- No commitment should be made to pay any witness in a trial before proceedings are fully concluded.

The Radio Authority goes further by stating that payment for interviews about seriously anti-social actions are also not allowed. This really resolves the debate for independent radio journalists over the payment to witnesses in notorious cases involving serial killers or well-known people. While the government contemplates introducing legislation to control such payments by newspaper and television media, the law for commercial radio journalists is already in place.

Interviewing criminals

The Radio Authority is anxious that radio journalists are fully conscious of the risks of interviewing criminals 'at large', individuals who advocate crime, or who are suspected of crime. When an interviewee is known to be wanted by the police or on the run from prison, radio journalists are liable to very serious charges if they impede apprehension or encourage the evasion of arrest.

Complaints

There are occasions when programmes cause offence to listeners. If complaints are received, they should be answered, however unpleasant it may be. There is always a temptation to dismiss the complaint, either mentally or verbally, as trivial and only the view of one listener. Don't.

If a listener is already annoyed enough to ring, and you act in an off-hand manner, you may lose that listener forever. The listener heard what you had to say, now it is your turn to listen.

You can often deal with a complaint either by explaining why something was done in a particular way, or listening politely to the complaint and then giving an assurance that the point has been taken. After all, sometimes listeners do make good points. If you have made a mistake, apologise and assure the listener that steps will be taken to ensure it will not happen again (and then take those steps).

On the other hand, do not let the listener dictate editorial policy. If a demand is made for 'equal time' or 'right of reply', deal with it sensitively but firmly. If you are not getting anywhere, ask the person to write. That not only gives you time to consider and consult, it also reduces the heat on both sides. But be sure to act on the letter when it does arrive.

If the complaint is serious, warn the management and consult them about how to handle it.

Apart from ringing us directly, listeners have access to two bodies which can receive and deal with complaints. The **Radio Authority** considers complaints about programmes, advertising and sponsorship and transmissions. If it proceeds with an investigation, it will ask for a tape of the item in question. If the programme is found to breach the Authority's rules, it can:

- admonish a station
- require a broadcast apology
- ask for a correction

- impose a fine
- shorten or revoke a station's licence.

The **Broadcast Standards Commission** (BSC) was set up in 1997 to replace and combine the areas of the British Complaints Commission, which considered complaints of unjust and infair treatment and infringement of privacy, and the Broadcast Standards Council, which concentrated on standards of taste, decency and the portrayal of sex and violence. After an inquiry, the BSC may require the publication of its findings.

Broadcasters have a duty to inform and stimulate debate in a responsible and objective manner, and within the bounds of good taste. In return we get some flimsy protection from the law, but generally we are on our own. On top of all this, we also have to entertain. Don't be daunted. Putting together good programmes is challenging, but it is also good fun.

CHAPTER 8
The law and the courts

Introduction

Most of us never get involved with the law and therefore know little about it. There is a sort of received wisdom that everything to do with the law is complicated and difficult to understand. While this may be so in some areas, generally the law and the way the administration of justice functions are logical and have more to do with common sense than you might expect.

Most of the following chapters concern the law and legal procedures in England and Wales. But several sections on the law in Scotland have been included. For more information about the different Scottish system consult the Law Society of Scotland.

Lawyers often use very precise language which is either not English or old-fashioned English. If there is confusion or doubt about the meaning of legal terminology, a good dictionary will explain it. The precision of legal language extends to the particular wording of a law, so it is important to read each word carefully.

Be sure that you understand these chapters on the law. As a journalist you have no special rights or privileges, so it is important to keep within the law and have it on your side. Journalists have fewer civil rights than ordinary citizens. As a journalist, if you antagonise the administration of justice you are not entitled to trial by jury. It is a strict liability offence. This means that the fact that you did not mean it, or did not intend to commit the offence is irrelevant. There is no limit to how much you can be fined. The maximum jail sentence is two years. You are prosecuted, convicted and sentenced by the legal profession – the very people you are accused of offending.

Divisions of the law

The criminal law deals with offences. When you see a case referred to as R v Smith it means that the state is prosecuting the case, the R standing for Rex or Regina (depending on whether it is in the reign of a king or queen) who is versus (against) Smith. Criminal cases must be proved 'beyond reasonable doubt'. They are prosecuted and the guilty punished, e.g. by a fine, imprisonment or probation.

There are two elements in most crimes: a criminal act and a guilty intent. Without intent, no crime is committed, unless the crime is 'absolute' (i.e. no intent is required, as in jumping a red light) or intent is presumed because it occurred through recklessness (as when an accident is caused by a speeding driver).

The civil law deals with claims of either a private or a public nature to remedy wrongs. Cases are referred to as, for example, Brown and Smith. The plaintiff (Brown) sues the defendant (Smith) who may be found liable. If you find it difficult to remember what each side is called, you may find it helpful to remember that it is the *plaint*iff who is making the com*plaint*. Civil cases must be proved 'on a balance of probability', which is less onerous than in criminal courts.

Types of courts

All cases must follow a prescribed route through the courts. A case starts in the lower courts, and may then progress through to successively higher courts as shown below.

Criminal courts	**Civil courts**
Magistrates Court	County Court
Crown Court	High Court
Court of Appeal	Court of Appeal
House of Lords	House of Lords

Criminal courts

Magistrates Courts

All criminal cases start in the Magistrates Courts, which always make the initial decisions about whether bail and/or legal aid will be granted, although lawyers sometimes challenge those decisions in a higher court. Most relatively minor cases do not proceed to a higher court.

Magistrates are usually lay men and women who rely on the clerk of the court to advise them on the law, but there are also legally qualified stipendiary magistrates who sit in some courts in larger cities. While lay magistrates usually sit in twos or threes, stipendiaries sit on their own. All magistrates are Justices of the Peace (JPs).

Cases in the Magistrates Courts fall into one of three categories. **Summary trials** must be heard in the Magistrates Court and cannot proceed to the Crown Court. These cases are relatively minor, e.g. obstructing the highway, motoring offences, minor public order offences such as obstructing a police officer, being drunk and disorderly, vagrancy, not paying the BBC television licence, gross indecency, prostitution. Magistrates also try hybrid offences which can also be heard in the Crown Court, such as theft and indecent assault; they process serious prosecutions as remands and committals and decide bail for remanded prisoners. Generally the maximum fine is £5,000 for one offence, the maximum prison sentence for one offence is 6 months and the maximum sentence for several offences is 1 year. Magistrates can decide to send a trial for a hybrid offence to the Crown Court despite election by the defendant to be tried in the lower court. Magistrates can also send convicted defendants for sentencing to the Crown Court following conviction for hybrid offences. Unless the magistrate is a stipendiary (i.e. legally qualified), at least two magistrates must sit in summary trials.

In cases **triable either way**, e.g. most offences of theft, damaging property, arson, bigamy, etc., the prosecution will first say where they think a case should be heard. If it is serious (e.g. theft of £10,000), the prosecution will opt for the Crown Court, and the magistrates will 'decline jurisdiction'. If the theft is of a can of beans, the prosecution will accept the magistrates' jurisdiction, but the defendant can exercise the right to trial by jury, which means opting for the Crown Court.

Serious charges, e.g. murder, rape, are **indictable only**, and must be tried by a jury, but these cases still pass through the Magistrates Court.

Any case that is progressing beyond the Magistrates Court must go through **committal proceedings**. In these cases, the role of the magistrates is to decide whether there is a case to answer, i.e. whether the prosecution's evidence is strong enough.

A 'paper committal' means that the prosecution and the defence agree that there is a case to answer based on papers served by the prosecution on the defence. This procedure was brought in to reduce the number of lengthy committal proceedings.

In an old style committal the defence insists that the prosecution present all or part of their evidence in open court in order to determine whether there is a case to answer. If the magistrates decide that there is, the case is sent to the Crown Court. If not, the defendant is discharged. In the latter case it is wrong to say that the defendant was 'found innocent'; you can say that the person was 'released' or 'discharged'. The most memorable challenge in recent years was the prosecution of the serial killer Rosemary West. The prosecution had to present its key evidence which was then tested by the defence by cross-examination in order to prove that there was not a prima facie case to justify trial by jury.

If someone is accused of serious fraud the case can be given a 'certificate' by the prosecution which will transfer it directly to the Crown Court without a lengthy committal.

The Magistrates Courts Act 1980 lays down strict reporting restrictions on all cases in the Magistrates Courts, unless it is the actual hearing of a summary case. (See below.) A defendant can ask to have the restrictions lifted.

Crown Courts

Crown Court judges are always legally qualified with at least ten years' experience and, unless they are hearing submissions or dealing with matters from the Magistrates Courts (e.g. sentencing), they sit with a jury. So long as reports are within the bounds of contempt of court, restrictions do not generally apply unless a judge specifically orders them.

There are eleven Crown Courts in London, including the Old Bailey, or Central Criminal Court. Cases can be transferred to the Old Bailey for security reasons, or because a defendant is thought to be unable to get a fair trial at a local Crown Court because of the strength of local opinion.

Circuit judges sit in criminal cases, while High Court judges can hear either criminal or civil cases. If it is a serious case, whether in the Old Bailey or any other Crown Court, a High Court judge may hear the case.

Court of Appeal

This court hears appeals from the Crown Courts only on points of law against conviction, or against sentence. Once a jury has heard and decided on a particular case, the Court of Appeal will be reluctant to overturn the jury's decision. But if the trial judge misdirected the jury on a point of law, or if the Court decides that fresh evidence might have brought a jury to a different conclusion, the Appeal Court can overturn a conviction, or more rarely order a re-trial.

It is not so unusual for the Court to hear appeals against sentence. If the defence thinks the sentence was too severe, an application can be made to the Court of Appeal to have it reduced, but the Court does have the option of increasing the sentence if it is so minded. Only the defence can appeal against conviction, but either side can appeal against sentence.

The prosecution can appeal against an acquittal, but the appeal must come from the Attorney General and the Court of Appeal's decision will not alter the trial court's outcome.

Thus the Court can deliberate on the general issues of a case, but cannot fine or jail the particular defendant.

Three appeal judges hear each case, and the majority decision is binding.

The Court of Appeal is usually the last opportunity to challenge a decision, because very few cases are accepted by the Lords.

House of Lords

Appeals only get to the Lords if they involve points of law that are of general public importance. The Lords will not hear a case unless both of those requirements have been met.

Cases are not heard by the whole House of Lords. There are nine Lords of Appeal who are paid, professional judges, holding life peerages. Five Lords hear each case, and a majority decision is binding.

Both the Court of Appeal and the House of Lords are said to 'grant leave to appeal', which means they have decided to hear the case. Otherwise 'leave is refused'.

Civil courts

County Courts

County Court judges sit on their own. They are legally qualified, and full judges must have at least 10 years' experience. County Courts deal with personal injury cases where damages do not exceed £50,000, or property valued at less than £30,000. Day-to-day cases are dealt with here, and County Courts deal with about 90 per cent of civil cases. The range of cases they hear is very broad, but a large part of their work involves landlord-and-tenant disputes and debt. Juries are now normally only introduced to decide the facts in civil actions in relation to libel actions or actions claiming wrongful arrest and malicious prosecution.

High Court

The High Court usually sits in the Royal Courts of Justice in the Strand, London. The judge sits alone, except for certain appeals, and his decision is not generally given directly the case finishes, but 'handed down' at some later date when he has considered the arguments. The decision is handed down in writing to the interested parties rather than spoken in court.

The High Court deals with cases involving sums higher than the County Courts can hear, and some sorts of cases, e.g. libel, start in the High Court.

While most cases are heard in London, High Court judges also 'go on circuit' and hear cases in other major cities.

Court of Appeal

This court also sits in the Royal Courts of Justice in the Strand. Appeals are generally heard by three judges, and the majority ruling is binding. They hear appeals from the County and High Courts, and from employment tribunals.

House of Lords

As in criminal cases, the Lords grant leave only on points of law that are of general public importance.

Judges' titles

Depending on seniority, different judges are referred to in particular ways.

- Magistrates are referred to as Mr, Mrs or Miss Smith.
- County Court judges are referred to as Judge Smith.
- Crown Court circuit judges are initially referred to as Judge John Smith, then subsequently as Judge Smith. High Court judges are Mr, Mrs or Miss Justice Smith.
- In the Court of Appeal, whether it is a civil or criminal case, judges are referred to as Lord Justice Smith. The title of Lord Justice applies to women as well as men.
- Regardless of whether it is a civil or criminal case, judges in the House of Lords are referred to as Lord Smith.

Solicitors and barristers

At the time of writing, the Lord Chancellor is proposing a shakeup in the system of court representation, which may blur the distinction between the roles of solicitors and barristers. At the moment, they perform different functions.

Solicitors see clients first and assess their cases. They can take advice from barristers at any stage, but it is the job of the solicitor to deal generally with the case and prepare it for court. They negotiate with 'the other side' when appropriate, decide which laws and precedents are pertinent, arrange witnesses and plan the trial strategy.

There are rules about which courts solicitors are allowed 'a right of audience' in, i.e. which courts allow them to speak. They are confined to speaking in the lower courts, such as Magistrates Courts, County Courts and tribunals. There are circumstances in which they are allowed to speak to a Crown Court, but generally they have to 'brief' a barrister for that stage.

In criminal cases, solicitors for the defence are usually in private practice, while those for the prosecution are usually part of the state Crown Prosecution Service or CPS.

Solicitors can practise alone or in partnerships. Barristers, on the other hand, are always self-employed and organise themselves to share 'chambers' (their office) and 'clerks' (who run their office).

Barristers (also called 'counsel') cannot solicit work directly from members of the public, and can only get their briefs from solicitors. They have a right of audience in all courts, although when they appear in Magistrates Courts, they do not wear black gowns and white wigs. Those come into play once a case gets to the Crown Court. Judges also wear gowns and wigs, although more senior judges' robes are red. When barristers have distinguished themselves in practice for a number of years, they may be appointed as a 'Queen's Counsel', or QC. QCs are always barristers.

A barrister may work closely with a solicitor in the planning of a case, or, if it is a straightforward hearing, may present the case simply on the basis of having read the documents.

Once a case gets to the Crown Court, the solicitor, or a representative of the solicitor, must always 'sit behind' counsel – a literal description of their respective positions.

Solicitors are answerable to the Law Society, while the equivalent for barristers is the Bar Council (when barristers qualify, they are 'called to the Bar').

During the course of a case, or at the end of it, the solicitor can make statements or be interviewed. Most barristers, however, refuse to talk about a case in which they are involved, and confine themselves to speaking about general issues of law.

Solicitors who have acquired full rights of audience for the requisite number of years would be eligible to become judges.

Court procedure

Criminal courts

The basic procedure in criminal courts is as follows:

1. The accused is read the charges ('charged' in Magistrates Courts; 'arraigned' in Crown Courts, which means it is an 'indictable' case) and asked to plead guilty or not guilty. If the plea is guilty points 2–7 are omitted. If not guilty:
2. The prosecution opens the case with a speech, then calls witnesses (who can be cross-examined by the defence) to prove the case.
3. The defence makes an opening statement, then calls witnesses (who can be cross-examined by the prosecution).
4. The prosecution makes a closing speech (except in the Magistrates Courts where the prosecution only replies to points of law).
5. The defence makes a closing speech.
6. In jury trials only the judge sums up the evidence and instructs the jury on points of law before the jury retires to consider their verdict.
7. If the defendant is found innocent he is acquitted. If he is found guilty or pleaded guilty in the first place (see 1 above):
8. The prosecution outlines relevant criminal records, reports, etc.
9. The defence sets out pleas in mitigation (reasons why the defendant should not get the harshest penalty).
10. Sentence is passed.

At the end of the prosecution's case (point 4 above), the defence may claim there is 'no case to answer'. If the court accepts this application, the case is discharged.

A jury is made up of 12 people, but if for some reason one, or even two, need to drop out during the course of a trial, the case will probably carry on so as not to cause the defendant the added stress of having to start all over again. The jury may agree a unanimous verdict, but if they are unable to agree, a majority verdict of 11–1 or 10–2 can be accepted by the judge. If the jury has been reduced, the judge can accept a 10–1 or 9–1 decision.

If a defendant is convicted by a majority jury decision, you can say so; but it is regarded as bad form to say that an acquittal was by majority (it suggests that some jurors thought the defendant was guilty).

Civil courts

The order in civil cases is similar:

1 The plaintiff's lawyer may make an opening speech (but this is not mandatory).
2 The plaintiff's lawyer calls witnesses (who can be cross-examined by the defence).
3 The defence lawyer makes an opening speech.
4 The defence calls witnesses (who can be cross-examined by the plaintiff's lawyer).
5 The defence lawyer makes a closing speech.
6 The plaintiff's lawyer makes a closing speech.
7 (In jury trials only) the judge sums up the evidence and directs the jury on points of law.
8 The judgment is given.

Types of crime

Never ascribe the wrong charge to a defendant. If, for example, you say someone is accused of robbery when in fact it is theft, expect a call from the defending lawyer, because you have just accused the defendant of a more serious crime than the prosecution has. These are some of the more newsworthy charges you may come across.

Crimes against the person

- Murder: killing with malice aforethought. Carries a mandatory life sentence.
- Manslaughter: killing without malice aforethought.
- Suicide: ceased to be a crime in 1961, but it is still a crime to assist suicide, unless it is a suicide pact.
- Infanticide: killing of a baby by its mother, whose responsibility may be reduced because her mind is disturbed by the stress of the birth.
- Assault: an act which puts someone in fear of an attack.
- GBH (grievous bodily harm): an attack with intent to cause serious bodily harm (maximum sentence life imprisonment).

- Malicious wounding: carries a sentence of up to 5 years' imprisonment.
- ABH (actual bodily harm): not as serious as GBH.
- Rape: sexual intercourse with penetration with a woman or man without their consent.
- Unlawful sexual intercourse: intercourse with a girl under 16.
- Indecent assault: an assault involving indecency (but not rape) which can be committed by a male or female against either sex, but if the person is under 16, consent is no defence.

Crimes against property

- Theft: stealing something with the intent of permanently depriving the owner.
- Robbery: theft by force or threat of force.
- Burglary: trespassing into a building and stealing or committing GBH, or intending to steal, or commit GBH, or rape.
- Aggravated burglary: armed burglary.
- Obtaining property by deception: can be called fraud.
- Obtaining a pecuniary advantage by deception: can also be called fraud (an example is someone obtaining an overdraft by deception).
- Blackmail: an 'unwarranted' demand with menaces.
- Handling: receiving, keeping or disposing of goods knowing or suspecting them to be stolen, or assisting another to do so.
- TCA: taking a car without authority: not to be confused with theft, You can say the car was taken for a joy ride, but not stolen. Colloquially known as 'twoccing' – taking without consent.

Motoring offences

- Causing death by reckless driving (maximum sentence 5 years).
- Reckless driving: driving without regard for other road users.
- Careless driving: driving without due care and attention. Less serious than reckless driving.
- Driving while unfit through drugs or drink.
- Driving over the limit: driving with excess alcohol in the blood.

Tribunals and inquiries

The workings and decisions of tribunals and inquiries are often newsworthy. They tend to operate in a less formal way than the courts, which can make reporting them easier. There are hundreds of different sorts of tribunals, each with its own working practices and powers, ranging from Mental Health Review Tribunals, which decide whether a person should be compulsorily detained under the Mental Health Act, to professional bodies, which can fine or suspend their members, to public inquiries held to investigate and report on the causes of major accidents. There is even a Wireless Telegraphy Tribunal, though it has never been convened since its inception in 1949.

Most tribunals and inquiries operate under quasi-legal procedures and your coverage of them will fall within privilege, although it will be qualified privilege in most cases. They tend to be open to the public and press, except for hearings into the misconduct of members of some professions (including the medical and legal professions), Mental Health Review Tribunals and Supplementary Benefit Tribunals. It is not clear whether tribunals and inquiries are legally courts and therefore covered by the rules of contempt, but practice and rulings to date suggest that contempt does not apply in most instances.

The only tribunals for which legal aid is available are the Mental Health Review Tribunal and the Lands Tribunal. For all the others, clients can get legal advice on legal aid, but the state will not pay for a lawyer to present the case itself. Given the complexity of the law covered by many tribunals, this has been heavily criticised. The body that keeps tribunals under review, the Council on Tribunals, has pressed governments for many years to extend legal aid, but so far without success.

The most likely sources of interesting stories are industrial tribunals, planning inquiries and public inquiries.

Industrial tribunals

Industrial tribunals decide on a wide range of employment matters, including claims of unfair dismissal, redundancy pay, sexual or racial discrimination, and issues relating to trade union representation. Three people hear cases: a chairperson (who is legally trained), a representative of a trade union and a representative of industry, although their affiliations are not made public.

Appeals go to the Employment Appeal Tribunal where a High Court judge sits with at least two lay people.

Planning inquiries

If for any reason a local authority refuses permission for land development or a change of its use, the applicant is entitled to a planning inquiry. Objectors are entitled to an inquiry only if the Secretary of State agrees to allow one, or if the objectors can show that a national issue is involved.

Strictly speaking, it is the Secretary of State for the Environment who takes the final decision on disputed planning appeals, but an inspector is usually appointed to head the inquiry, and the inspector will hear arguments from the applicant and objectors and then present recommendations to the Secretary of State, or, in some cases, decide the issue. The only appeal is by submission to the Secretary of State.

Public inquiries

A major disaster or crisis will often provoke a public inquiry. These may be set up by a government department (as with the Taylor inquiry into the Hillsborough disaster), or by a private organisation. Public inquiries tend to be quasi-judicial in nature, but the legal powers available to them depend upon how they were constituted in the first place. Royal Commissions and departmental inquiries command far more powers than private inquiries, which depend on the good will of participants.

Public inquiries produce reports from which the government decides whether to take any further action.

Coroner's courts

If a death is unnatural, violent or sudden, a coroner's inquest must be held. If the autopsy subsequently shows that the person died of natural causes, the coroner can dispense with the inquest.

A coroner can be a barrister, solicitor or doctor of at least five years' standing. If the coroner is not legally qualified, the inquest will be assisted by a policeman who acts as the coroner's officer.

The coroner can decide whether to have a jury unless the death was in prison, by poison or in circumstances prejudicial to public safety, in which case a jury must sit. Juries consist of between 7 and 11 members, and they return a verdict. If the coroner is sitting without a jury, a verdict is recorded.

If a crime is associated with the death, the coroner will formally open an inquest and then adjourn it until after any proceedings involved in the crime have finished.

Inquests are always open to reporters and the general public, unless considerations of national security make it necessary to hold the inquest in camera (in secret).

Coroner's courts are inquisitorial rather than accusatorial. The coroner does not act as an impartial judge. He or she decides which witnesses should be called and leads the parties through their testimony. Lawyers for interested parties can be present and can be allowed to ask questions, but they do not make opening or closing statements.

The purpose of the inquest is to establish the identity of the person who has died, and how, when and where the death occurred. If a jury is hearing the case, they can only return a verdict on how the death occurred. They are not allowed to name anyone in connection with murder or manslaughter.

Reports of coroner's inquests carry the protection of absolute privilege.

Treasure trove

If gold or silver is found and the rightful owners or their descendants cannot be established, a coroner's inquest will be opened to decide whether the person who found it can keep it, or whether it is treasure trove. Treasure trove is the property of the Crown.

The definition of treasure trove is property which the last owner intended to recover. If it was deliberately abandoned or accidentally lost, it is not treasure trove. So, for instance, if coins are found at the site of an ancient religious site or burial ground, and the prevailing view is that those coins were sacrifices or offerings, it is unlikely that they would be deemed treasure trove.

Since the advent of metal detectors, there has been a spate of treasure trove cases, and they are almost always good human interest stories. The reason these cases are heard in the Coroner's court reflects the original purpose of the coroner: to protect the Crown's financial interests.

European courts

European courts can influence British courts, but courts in this country must always follow British law. There are two European courts which influence our laws. Their proceedings are not covered by privilege.

The **European Court of Justice** is part of the European Union (EU), and it will hear only cases that have been referred to it by a member state. Its decisions are binding on British courts, but only cases which involve questions of European law are heard here.

Newsworthy cases often find their way to the **European Court of**

Human Rights, which is part of the Council of Europe. The decisions of this court are not strictly speaking binding on British courts, but since this country is a signatory to the Convention on Human Rights, the government has a responsibility to amend the law in accordance with its findings.

If a defendant claims that any section of the Convention has been contravened, the European Commission of Human Rights will consider the case only when all domestic remedies have been exhausted (i.e. the case has failed in all possible appeals, right up to the House of Lords). If the Commission agrees that the defendant has a possible case, it will invite both sides to try to find a mutually agreed conclusion. Failing an agreement, the Commission may pass on the case to be heard in full in the European Court of Human Rights.

Alternatively, if there is no domestic remedy available, a case can be started by the defendant making a complaint (or submission) in writing directly to the Commission. If the Commission accepts that the complaint is worth consideration, it will first invite the two sides to try to work out a solution. If no solution is forthcoming, the issue will go to the Court of Human Rights to be heard in full.

European law

At the time of writing, the government was in the process of incorporating the Convention of Human Rights into UK legislation. The Home Secretary Jack Straw told the House of Commons that the government intended to ensure that the Human Rights Act would give greater weight to freedom of expression rights under the European Convention than to privacy rights.

The Scottish system

There are some essential differences in the Scottish legal system. In Scotland, barristers are called advocates. There is a 'not proven' verdict. There is a rule requiring the trial of persons to be brought within a 110 day period. The accused in serious criminal trials is called 'the panel'. In Scotland the prosecutors do not begin with an opening speech, unlike in England and Wales.

In Scotland, sheriff courts and district courts deal with lesser offences in what is known as 'summary jurisdiction'. The proceedings are based around 'a complaint' and the jury does not sit in judgment, but is decided by Justices of the Peace or professional Stipendiaries. The more serious crimes are heard in the sheriff courts and the High Court of Justiciary in a process known as 'solemn jurisdiction'. Proceedings are based around an 'indictment' and a jury of 15 people have the responsibility of judging the facts in dispute.

The District courts can only fine up to £1,000 and/or impose 60 days' imprisonment. The Sheriff Courts deal with most criminal cases in Scotland. They operate in six sheriffdoms:

1 Grampian, Highland and Islands
2 Tayside, Central and Fife
3 Lothian and Borders
4 Glasgow and Strathkelvin
5 North Strathclyde, and
6 South Strathclyde, Dumfries and Galloway.

Trials are presided over by the sheriff or the sheriff principal. They have to be lawyers of ten years' standing and can try cases of solemn and summary jurisdiction. Murder, treason and rape have to be tried at the High Court of Justiciary. Powers of punishment are restricted to 3 months' imprisonment for summary cases and 3 years' imprisonment for solemn cases heard with a jury. All prosecutions are conducted by the Procurator-Fiscal in Scotland or his or her number two, known as 'depute'.

The High Court of Justiciary tries the most serious criminal prosecutions in Scotland and has sole jurisdiction for murder, treason and rape. The judicial hierarchy consists of the Lord Justice-General (same person as the Lord President of the Court of Session) the Lord Justice-Clerk and 24 Lords Commissioners of Justiciary. They are the equivalent of English and Welsh High Court Judges. The seat of this court is Parliament House in Edinburgh. It also goes on circuit around Scotland. The prosecutions are conducted by the Lord Advocate, Solicitor-General or Advocate-Depute. This court hears appeals from courts of summary jurisdiction. Appeals from solemn jurisdiction trials go to the High Court of Justiciary sitting as a Court of Criminal Appeal. At least three judges sit to hear appeals against conviction and sentence. This is the highest criminal court in Scotland and cases cannot go to the House of Lords from this point.

There are a number of other differences between Scotland and the rest of Britain. For example youths/children are aged under 16 whereas in England and Wales they are 17 and under. There is no statutory prohibition on identifying sexual offence complainants in Scotland but as a matter of custom nothing is published which could lead to their identification unless they give their permission. Judges in the High Court of Justiciary normally direct the public to leave when rape complainants give evidence but allow reporters to remain on the basis that there will not be any identification. The Scottish Judges have the power to direct non publication of witnesses' names but rarely exercise it because Scottish journalists have maintained a voluntary code of discretion on identifying rape victims. This is a major contrast to England and Wales where statutory prohibition exists for all time once an accusation has been made. The rape complainant still has to give evidence in open court before the public gallery and with his or her identity revealed and referred to during the proceedings.

In England and Wales bail applications at Magistrates Courts are held in open court. In Scotland they are always in private.

Committals

The preliminary enquiry by justices to evaluate the appropriateness of committing indictable offences for trial at the Crown Court does not happen in Scotland. In contrast, the first appearance of a person facing solemn jurisdiction is in private before the sheriff. Furthermore the only preliminary court process in Scotland can take the form of a judicial examination or discovery of information from the accused. The Procurator-Fiscal tests an incriminating statement. This process is not public.

CHAPTER 9

Court reporting

General advice

Reporting the legal system is not just a matter of trying to avoid stepping on anti-personnel mines. Journalists should always understand the value of establishing excellent sources so that your lines of communication are so good you can anticipate trouble before it turns into formal legal problems and you can also be ahead of the competition in the field of broadcast news coverage. You must do everything you can to build sources that go beyond office hour contacts. The home numbers of key personnel and the confidential links you have with people who have a protagonist role in this field will enable you to confirm and corroborate accuracy and be guided on the perspective and importance of developments.

Important sources

The court staff

Take a lot of effort to establish good contacts with the key personnel in list offices at court complexes. The Lord Chief Justice of England and Wales at the time of writing, Sir Thomas Bingham, recently directed that there should be at least one individual in court buildings who is able and willing to help the media. Widen the range of contacts to include liaison with barristers, judges and coroners. From the point of view of professional etiquette they will not be able to go on the record, but reliable and trustworthy relations will improve legal understanding of the needs of broadcasting, and retirement or public issue stories could lead to exclusive interviews. The Kilmuir Rule established in the 1950s banning judges from giving media interviews has been relaxed. Judges can enter discussions on general issues. Barristers and QCs can now be interviewed about their cases. Radio is the ideal medium to achieve that. Effective contacts can be established through public and charitable events, or through the generation of soft feature coverage.

The Court Reporting Agency

All independent radio newsrooms depend on freelance agencies covering courtroom complexes for tip-offs and copy. Newsroom budgets are small so the newsdesk will normally receive copy written for a variety of outlets and normally orientated for the newspaper medium. It is vital to establish an effective relationship and understanding of the local court reporting agencies. Assess their infrastructure and experience. Evaluate their strengths and weaknesses so that you can judge the extent to which the copy is accurate and reliable. If you are pro-active in going to meet the agencies, are efficient in ensuring payment for contributions, you will find that the freelance stringers and agencies will respond enthusiastically with a plentiful and rich supply of material. In a competitive environment you want the local agencies to think of you first when they are across a significant story.

Police

Investigating officers will be closer to the nuances of an investigation than anyone else. Establishing trustworthy journalist/source relationships is vital and will be rewarding as the officers progress in their careers to positions of greater responsibility.

Police Public Relations Bureau

Trust and professional familiarity with every aspect of police public relations means that the flow of official information will be fast and accurate.

Solicitors

Most news organisations neglect establishing good and fulfilling relations with the foot soldiers of defence and representation in the legal system. The same amount of effort and priority should be given to solicitor contacts as is given to police contacts. Solicitors feel more vulnerable and isolated when outside the shield of public relations machinery that is normally present in county and metropolitan constabularies. If you are courteous and trustworthy you will find that lawyer contacts are invaluable.

The Crown Prosecution Service and Procurator-Fiscal

These are the people who will be handling the prosecution after the police enquiry. They tend to be neglected by journalists and an effort to establish good communication will mean that you will be well informed of the progress of prosecution preparation and presentation.

The ordinary or extraordinary people who are directly involved in the case

The more unusual, socially and politically significant or sensational the case, the less likely you will be able to maintain a direct communication in this area. National newspaper editors and the 'media pack' syndrome have a detrimental effect on the willingness of people at the centre of a case to communicate their story and feelings. The media are now much more competitive. People can say more on the radio and it is a more friendly medium. There is no question of any money being paid or expected. If you show honesty and genuine sympathy and respect you can establish relationships which transcend the ugly dimensions of competitive media interest in a crime/legal story.

Reporting the criminal courts

Some basic rules on attitude and approach are offered here.

1 The environment

The first thing a radio journalist should watch out for is psychological intimidation and any feeling of insecurity about not being able to cope with legal restrictions that dog the criminal justice process. This means the reporter has to develop a confident understanding of what not to do and a basic knowledge of media law.

2 Dress smartly

It helps to dress smartly. Untidy, unconventional and avant-garde dress only serves to draw attention to yourself. Some officials will perceive this as provocation and disrespect. In addition, witnesses and victims' relatives may not take kindly to exhibitionism. The courtroom process is very much like a religious ceremony. Society is going through a catharsis of accusation, trial, judgment and punishment.

3 Establish point of communication

Establish your telephone point. Be clear in your mind where you will be filing from. Find out about ISDN points and public telephones. Make sure that they work. If you are going to croc-clip a news transmission, find a friendly office or shop so that you can plug in your telephone adaptor and reverse the charges. If you are using a cellular phone make sure there is an area you can use where the signal power is good for broadcast. If you are using a radio car, make sure you are not breaching parking regulations. You do not want to find that the car has been towed away after the end of the case. You also want to avoid collecting parking tickets.

4 Avoid unnecessary rows with petty officials

Courtroom complexes have a plethora of men and women who tend to be prejudiced against journalists. Do not waste energy and time fighting them. Make sure you have valid reporters' identification. There is now a nationally approved press pass recognised by all police forces which is essential for getting into the Old Bailey. In the absence of this make sure that you have a letter of accreditation from the news editor which can be checked. Smile and be pleasant and ignore rude behaviour.

Most courtroom complexes will not allow you to take your recorder/camera/microphones into the courtroom. In any case in England and Wales the 1925 Administration of Justice Act prohibited the use of cameras on the court precincts. This does not apply to sound recording equipment. For the sake of peace and quiet it is not worth arguing about the alleged illegality of simply possessing the equipment. Leave it at the main desk or reception or with a nearby and trustworthy shop-owner.

In fact the 1981 Contempt of Court Act only makes radio journalists in contempt of court if they use the recorder inside the courtroom without the leave of the court, or bring the machine into a courtroom with the intention of using it. Court officials would have to have evidence that a reporter intended to use it inside.

There should be no restriction on using recorders on courtroom precincts, i.e. within the courtroom building or in the corridors. It is very useful to record interviews in those situations when the press people are firing questions. According to the Contempt of Court Act a courtroom has to be a 'body exercising the judicial power of the state'. By no stretch of the imagination can a courtroom corridor, or lobby be included in this definition. However, judges, magistrates and their officials have judged it to be so. As a result of this policy radio reporters were banned from using their recorders outside the courts at the Old Bailey from 1996. No such ban is applied in the same circumstances at the Royal Courts of Justice in the Strand. Again for peace of mind and to avoid having your equipment unlawfully seized and your reporting function disrupted, take up the choice of doing the interview outside the building with the television people.

5 Courtroom etiquette

Try to be like a chameleon. Do not do anything that draws attention to yourself. Enter and leave courtrooms quietly. Do not pass between speaking barristers and judge/magistrates when they are sitting. Walk behind the rows of solicitors and police officers. Try to use the press bench. Try to find a location within the courtroom so that you can hear clearly, and have something to rest your notebook and pen on. Do not use your cellphone when a court is sitting. Do not forget to switch off your cellphone and bleeper when inside the courtroom. Make sure your watch alarm does not go off when you are inside a courtroom. If you have a sore throat and tendency to cough take in some cough sweets. Do not make a visible show of laughing or showing an emotional reaction to what is heard and what happens during the course of a trial. This is open to misinterpretation by all sides and will undermine your credibility. You are not obliged to bow obsequiously to the judge/magistrates when they enter and leave the courtroom. Only 'officers of the court', i.e. barristers, police officers and solicitors, are under this obligation in terms of etiquette.

6 Notebook discipline

Keep a tidy and accurate notebook. Date, time and locate each court case. It is useful to have shorthand, but polyglot and fast longhand styles can get you by. You will find that facts and points are often repeated in the laborious process of adversarial trial. You will need the help of your reporting colleagues during a fast sentence and comparing notes is a useful process of ensuring accuracy. Be helpful, respectful and friendly to other journalists covering a case. Despite competitive pressures journalists need each other because it is impossible to be in the right place all of the time. Try to write your voice reports and copy stories while in the courtroom, on a separate sheet of paper. This means that you do not risk missing important evidence, or developments while you are outside the courtroom filing.

7 Conduct inside and outside court

Avoid expressing your opinion or facts about the case within earshot of jurors, lawyers, police officers, defendants, witnesses and relatives. This could be a contempt of court, leading to the premature end of the case. It would also undermine your independent and journalistic credibility with the various parties to a case.

CHAPTER 10

Libel

Anything published through independent radio broadcasting in the UK has the risk of being a libel under the 1952 and 1996 Defamation Acts. Libel is a very complex area of the law. The odds are stacked against journalists and the inhibitions created by the threat of massive libel damages or very expensive litigation probably have a greater impact on freedom of expression in Britain than any other area of the law. Libel is determined by case law and very vague language in a few statutes. Because it depends on a subjective interpretation of 'ordinary meaning' at the time a jury considers the alleged libel, something actionable in 1959 could be a compliment in 1999.

There are aspects of the 1996 Defamation Act which still need time for case law testing before journalists can be altogether clear of how the land lies. For example, the new Act provides judges with the power to dispose of a libel action summarily and in favour of the person suing with no regard to the wishes of the defendant. This can be done where a judge decides that the defending media organisation has no realistic prospect of success and there is no other reason why the claim should go to trial. The maximum amount awarded in these circumstances is £10,000.

The courts mainly rely on previous cases (precedents) for guidance, while looking at each case on its own merits. Juries decide on the outcome of each case and the amount of damages that should be awarded, and they sometimes come to unexpected decisions.

Libel has been called a rich man's sport, because the legal costs together with any damages which may be awarded can make libel cases very expensive. Most libel cases are therefore settled out of court in order to hold down those costs.

This is an area of the law which challenges and sometimes confounds even the greatest legal minds. This chapter explains some of the basic principles of libel, so that you can avoid the more obvious pitfalls. As a broadcaster you must be aware of the scope of libel law and know something about the protection the courts have given journalists. Respect the law, but do not let it paralyse you.

What is libel?

Libel is the written publication of defamatory matter, while slander is the spoken word. Under the Defamation Acts of 1952 and 1996, the broadcasting of words was deemed to be a publication in permanent form, so broadcasters commit libel even though the words are spoken.

There is such a thing as criminal libel, but cases which fall into that category are extremely rare. Almost all libel cases are civil cases, so this chapter discusses only civil libel.

The law of libel has two purposes: to protect an individual's reputation and to preserve the right of free speech. These two purposes are by definition contradictory, and the law tries to find a fair balance between them.

A radio station is responsible for publishing any libel it broadcasts, no matter who said it or when. The courts do not care whether it was a reporter who uttered the defamatory words or an interviewee, the publisher has to answer for it, and in this case that means the station and you, if you are the reporter, presenter, producer or editor.

If there is an accusation of libel, a judge first has to decide whether the words broadcast were capable of being libellous. If the answer to that question is yes, then the case may go to a jury who will decide whether the words were defamatory.

Libel has been defined by the courts over the years. It is anything to a person's discredit, or which could:

- expose anyone to hatred, ridicule or contempt;
- cause anyone to be shunned or avoided;
- lower anyone in the estimation of right-thinking members of society generally;
- disparage anyone in their business, trade, office or profession.

Thus libel falls into two broad categories – people injured in their private reputation, and people injured in their business or professional reputation. It is not unusual for a plaintiff to bring an action alleging breaches in both categories.

Any statement that could lower the estimation of someone in the way he or she carries on a business, trade, office, or profession is libellous.

A statement that adversely affects someone's business is not necessarily libellous. Libel concerns people and their reputations. To be libellous, a statement must at least impute discreditable conduct or show that someone is ill suited or insufficiently qualified for that business or profession.

For example, it is libellous to report incorrectly that a doctor has been suspended by the BMA or is a quack. Both reports reflect adversely on the doctor's professional abilities. It is not libellous, however, to report that a doctor has retired from practice when that is not the fact. He may lose a lot of money as a result of the second statement, but it does not suggest that he is not good at his job. He may have a case for some sort of action, but not for libel.

It is libellous to report that someone is insolvent or in financial difficulties when that is not the case, even if you have not imputed any blame. People's financial standing is regarded as part of their reputation.

It does not have to be proved that a statement has discredited someone, only that a 'reasonable person' might think it could have that effect. This 'reasonable person' features heavily in libel cases, and has changed over the years. The sort of standards which applied in the 1920s do not necessarily apply now, and the reasonable person is what the jury decides is modern and moderate in outlook.

The courts have also said that this reasonable person should be allowed 'a certain amount of loose thinking', i.e. is not necessarily trained to think logically or listen to broadcasts carefully.

A libel action will fail if the statement has lowered someone only in the estimation of a particular group of people. It has to be in the minds of 'right thinking members of society generally'.

The meaning of words is crucial in the law of libel. The 'reasonable person' test is applied to the construction of the words by a judge in considering whether there is a case to answer, and then it is up to the jury to decide the natural and ordinary meaning of those words. Whatever sense or meaning might have been intended is irrelevant.

Deciding the meaning of words or phrases will also take into account any inference, implication or innuendo accepted by the 'reasonable' listener. It does not matter what witnesses or parties in the case think the words mean, the jury decides what 'reasonable people' might understand them to mean.

It also does not matter whether the person hearing the libel does not believe it is true. Even if the statement was broadcast as a joke, and witnesses are called to say they took it as a joke, the jury can still decide that it is libellous.

Every repetition of a libel is considered a fresh publication, so there may be cause for an action every time a libellous recording goes out, or if an apology for libel repeats the libel itself.

In January 1997, the BBC had to make its third public apology over the same libellous allegations that related to events in the 1970s. In 1982 and 1984 the corporation had to apologise at the High Court to Grunwick Processing Laboratories Ltd and George Ward, co-founder and managing director of the company, over broadcast claims that the company subjected employees to appalling working conditions and inadequate pay. The 1997 apology was offered for comments made by Jack Dromey, secretary of the Transport and General Workers' Union, in June 1996 on a Radio Five Live programme called 'Flashback'. Mr Ward and Grunwick were particularly aggrieved that the untrue allegations were broadcast again.

Remember that the station is responsible for any libel it puts to air, so it does not matter who first made the offending statement or how important that person is. If the station broadcasts a libellous statement, the station is as liable as the person who said it.

Proof

For a libel action to succeed, a plaintiff must prove that:

- the statement is defamatory, and
- it is reasonable for it to be understood to refer to the plaintiff, and
- it was published by the defendants.

The plaintiff does not have to prove:

- that the statement is false (although if it can be proved as true, that is a valid defence);
- intent: in many other areas of law, intent must be proved, but in libel the courts will presume intent (except in an 'unintentional' defence);
- that any real damage has been done: it is sufficient that a statement tends to discredit the plaintiff.

It is a mistake to think that you can avoid a libel action simply by not naming someone. If the plaintiff can satisfy a jury that the 'reasonable person' would make an identification 'based on the other material in the report, the case is proved.

Identification does not have to be explicit. It can be implicit. So if you say that police officers at a particular station sexually assaulted a suspect's girlfriend and there are only ten officers working from that station, they will all sue. The law is vague about when an identifiable group cannot all sue for the same allegation. But it would be wise to assume that an identifiable group can be anything under 20.

Not naming someone can create other problems. A local paper once quoted from a report by the district auditor which criticised the deputy housing manager on the local council. They did not name him, but were successfully sued by the new deputy housing manager who had taken over since the time dealt with by the report.

Defences to libel

At this stage, you must be thinking there is really nothing you can put to air without ending up in the High Court (which is where all libel cases are heard). This is where the law tries to strike the balance between protecting people's reputations and maintaining free speech.

There are seven recognised rejoinders to a plaintiff's initial claim of a libel. The first three are repudiations, the best and most final of which is the first one, but if a potential defendant can prove any one of the seven, or a combination of them, a libel case may not get past the lawyers' offices.

- The item was not broadcast by us.
- The words did not refer to the plaintiff, and could not be understood to do so.
- The words did not bear, and could not be understood to bear, a defamatory meaning.
- The words broadcast were authorised by the plaintiff, or consent had been given.
- The broadcast was privileged.
- The words were true in substance and fact.
- The words were fair comment on a matter of public interest.

If a possible libel goes out on air, tell the management as soon as possible and give them a recording to keep in case the libelled person threatens action. Much can be accomplished on the legal side so long as the station is seen to have acted quickly.

Keep conversations with potential plaintiffs short and encourage them to write. Listen carefully to what they say and make notes of the conversation. Never admit anything, even if you think they may be right. Tell them that you are not in a position to reply and that if they feel strongly they should write.

Of the seven rejoinders listed above, the last three are defences that are often used in libel trials. Their proper designations are privilege, justification and fair comment, the last two of which are very common defences. We will look at them in more detail below, as well as the defence of unintentional libel, but there are a further five defences of which you should be aware.

- The plaintiff has died. A dead person cannot be libelled (except in criminal libel), and even if someone has started an action, the case cannot carry on after his or her death.
- The plaintiff agreed to publication. This corresponds to the fourth rejoinder listed above, and would probably require a signed statement.

- Proceedings were not started within one year of publication. This is called the Statute of Limitation. Note it says started within one year. (Once a case does get going, it can take as long as a couple of years to get to court.)
- The matter has already been adjudged. Once the case has been decided, the only way a new case can be brought is if the statement is re-broadcast.
- Accord and satisfaction. This means that the plaintiff has accepted what has been done as sufficient, e.g. a correction and apology. Never assume you have got accord and satisfaction. Your lawyers will tell you when you have.

The five main defences

- Justification
- Fair comment
- Privilege
- Accord and satisfaction
- Unintentional libel

1 Justification

Apart from certain exceptions under the Rehabilitation of Offenders Act, it is a total defence to a libel action if a report can be proved to be true in substance and in fact.

This defence is far more difficult than it may look, because not only do you have to prove the precise truth of each statement broadcast, you also have to prove a reasonable interpretation of the words and any 'innuendo' that might be attached to them. However, in certain circumstances a defence of justification can succeed even if there are some inaccuracies within a report which is otherwise correct. The Defamation Act 1952 says that 'In an action for libel or slander in respect of words containing two or more distinct charges against the plaintiff, defence of justification shall not fail by reason only that the truth of every charge is not proved, if the words not proved to be true do not materially injure the plaintiff's reputation, having regard to the truth of the remaining charges.'

It has also been held that a man cannot claim damages for a character which he did not possess or deserve.

But these are the only real chinks in an otherwise difficult defence. Proving the exact truth of every statement may be possible, but the 'reasonable interpretation' is a minefield. There was a case just after the war, for example, when a local councillor's house appeared to be getting preferential treatment for official renovation work. Even though the local paper checked all the facts very carefully and could later prove them in court, they lost the case because the inference was that the councillor had secured preferential treatment.

The defence of justification is usually considered dangerous because the court may take a dim view of a persistence in it if it ultimately fails, and the jury may also award larger damages for the same reason. This happened in 1987 when Jeffrey Archer sued the *Star* for publishing an article linking him with a prostitute. He was awarded £500,000 damages after the judge told the jury that the paper had carried on to the bitter end, and if they found in Archer's favour, they should give sufficient damages to 'send a message to the world' that the accusation was false.

In 1987 the commercial radio station in Liverpool, Radio City, lost a libel case over a one hour documentary programme with the jury making an award amounting to £350,000. The programme featured interviews with four people who criticised the quality of holidays provided at a site in France by local businessman David Johnson. He gathered evidence showing that the great majority of his customers were content. An interviewer in the programme was heard to say 'We have spoken to literally dozens of people who bought holidays off you during the last two years and they have described you as a con man.' The problem with this question is that Mr Johnson could claim that the broadcast had the ordinary meaning that he was habitually dishonest or cynical towards his customers. This was a battle of justification, with the radio station producing 19 witnesses and the businessman providing 21. The case illustrates that the onus of proof in justifying libel broadcasts rests with the defendant.

2 Fair comment

Under this defence the words broadcast must be 'fair comment made without malice on some matter of public interest' and the facts which provoked the comment must be true. 'Public interest' has been held to include:

- The public conduct of anyone who holds or seeks a public office or position of trust
- Political and State matters (but we are constrained in this by parts of the Broadcasting Act and the RPA)
- Church matters
- The administration of justice
- The administration of local affairs by local authorities
- Anything which may be fairly said to invite comment or challenge public attention. This is a sort of catch-all section which would

include books, pictures, works of art, places and species of public entertainment, public performers, actors, singers, dancers.

'Fair comment' does not have to be proved to be true – comment is not capable of being either true or false. But what does have to be shown is that the comment was on established facts in the report and represents an honestly held opinion. The facts must be stated in the piece so the listener has some basis on which to assess whether comment is well-founded. The judge and jury do not have to share those opinions, but they have to be convinced that they are honestly held.

This defence will not succeed, however, if there was an imputation of corrupt or dishonourable motives which are not soundly proved. In other words, the law says you can think what you like and publish strong views on matters of public interest, but you cannot suggest someone is 'base or wicked'. The 'comment' has to be one that any person, even if prejudiced or obstinate, could honestly hold. The objective test is whether any 'fair-minded' person could honestly express that opinion on the proved facts.

Comment must also be recognisable as such and not so mixed up with facts or statements that it is difficult for the listener to distinguish fact from comment.

The only time fair comment can succeed if it is based on incorrect 'facts' is if those 'facts' arose in privileged circumstances (e.g. in Parliament or a court).

3 Privilege

There are circumstances in which, under the protection of privilege, the publication of defamatory matter is allowed. Privilege is one of the most important protections offered to journalists. Without it, it would not be possible to report fully on what happens in the courts, Parliament, local councils or most of the bodies which are part of our democratic process.

Under the protection of privilege, any action for libel will fail if the broadcast was a fair and accurate report of:

- Parliament, its committees, or papers (reports, papers, votes and proceedings).
- Judicial proceedings; judicial proceeding abroad outside the Commonwealth.
- Bodies recognised by law and exercising a quasi-judicial function, e.g. recognised tribunals, commissions, or inquiries set up by government departments.
- The findings or decision of any association formed to promote or

safeguard art, science, religion, learning, trade, industry, business, a profession, game, sport or pastime which is empowered by its constitution to control or adjudicate over its members. This covers bodies like the FA, Law Society, BMA, or Jockey Club. Note that privilege covers only the findings or decision, not a report.
- A public meeting lawfully held for a lawful purpose and for the furtherance of discussion of any matter of public concern, whether admission to the meeting is general or restricted (say, by buying a ticket).
- Any local authority or committee, and meeting of JPs or Justices acting otherwise than as a court, any tribunal, board, committee or body constituted by or under an Act of Parliament (such as an industrial tribunal).
- A general meeting of any public company.
- Any notice or statement issued by a government department, officer of state, local authority or chief of police. (The category does not cover leaked documents.)

The 1996 Defamation Act has added fair and accurate reports of bodies described above from anywhere in the world.

Comments made by press officers are not covered by privilege.

(a) Absolute privilege

Absolute privilege is enjoyed by, for instance, Members of Parliament who can say whatever they want during proceedings in the House of Commons without fear of action by the courts. It does not matter whether a statement was true or false, nor whether it was said maliciously. The 1688 Bill of Rights says: 'The freedom of speech and debates or proceedings in Parliament ought not to be impeached or questioned in any Court or place out of Parliament.'

The three words fair, accurate and contemporaneous should be stressed. 'Fair and accurate' does not necessarily mean it has to be a verbatim report. As long as it is fair, you can summarise what went on. Contemporaneous means exactly what it says if you are to claim absolute privilege, e.g. if a libel goes out while Parliament is being broadcast live. In follow-up reports you are covered by qualified privilege.

So far as reporting what happens in the courts is concerned, even though Parliament meant journalists to have only qualified privilege in the Libel Amendment Act 1888, the wording of the Act actually gives us absolute privilege (except in certain sorts of cases or courts, such as those involving juveniles). In order to hold on to this, the law specifies that the report must be fair and accurate. The report can therefore be as short as you like provided it gives a summary of both sides, contains no inaccuracies and does not give disproportionate weight to one side. Obviously, during the course of a trial, you cannot present both sides when you are reporting, say, the prosecution's opening speech. But by the end of the trial you should have redressed the balance. You should also underline your uneven approach by telling the listener that the trial is continuing.

Contemporaneous, in newspaper terms, means the first edition possible; in radio terms, it means the first opportunity for the report to be broadcast in a news bulletin or programme. All repetitions of the report are covered by qualified privilege.

If your report contains any inaccuracies, you lose all the protection offered by privilege. If you get a name wrong, or summarise the charges wrongly, the law will turn against you rather than help you. Take care, too, when writing cues for court reports. Do not include anything that could be seen as a misrepresentation or exaggeration, and do not present allegations as though they are proven facts.

(b) Qualified privilege

This defence affords almost as much protection as absolute privilege, so long as the report is fair and accurate. The main difference is that you must not be motivated by malice in your reporting.

Whenever this book refers to malice, it means what the law calls 'express malice', which in legal terms means more than just spite or ill-will. It covers any dishonest or improper motive, knowing a statement was not true, or being 'reckless' with the truth, which means neither considering nor caring about the truth.

Note that unlike absolute privilege, qualified privilege does not have to be contemporaneous, but you must take particular care if you are using information from, say, a cutting of an old court case – privilege does not apply as fully without this third element.

Qualified privilege also offers spokespeople the opportunity for 'explanation or contradiction'. If, for instance, a controversial statement was made by a shareholder during a general meeting of a public company, you would be covered by qualified privilege in reporting it, but someone from the company could insist on an explanation or contradiction being broadcast, if you did not cover it in your report.

Explanation or contradiction means that you have to give the target of any allegation the chance to put his or her side of the story. The new legislation in the 1996 Defamation Act provides qualified privilege for the first time for reports of overseas legal proceedings outside the Commonwealth. Without this protection there would not have been anything to stop British nurses Deborah Parry and Lucille McLauchlan suing UK news organisations reporting the continued Saudi Arabian government assertion that they were both guilty of murdering Australian nurse Yvonne Gilford.

The 1996 Defamation Act has added two further categories to the class of qualified privilege subject to comment and contradiction. The schedule now includes copies of documents circulated among shareholders of a UK public company created by statutory provision, and reports of findings and decisions of associations in the UK formed to promote charitable objects 'or objects beneficial to the community'.

The new act also includes police functions under the section 'Statements privileged subject to explanation or contradiction'.

4 Accord and satisfaction

This is a defence where the matter has been dealt with as a result of an agreement between the radio station and person complaining. This normally involves the publication of a correction and apology and this has been accepted by the plaintiff as a settlement of the complaint. Such a process would have to be handled by the senior management with the direct consultation of lawyers. Do not under any circumstances apologise and make immediate on-air corrections after receiving a solicitor's letter. Seek specialist legal advice. If you want to discuss an issue with a solicitor, do it on the basis that what you say is 'without prejudice' and write this on any correspondence you send to the lawyer and repeat the qualifying expression while talking to him on the phone.

A House of Lords ruling in 1993 established that institutions of local and national government cannot sue for libel in relation to their governmental and administrative functions. The Law Lords felt that in an action between Derbyshire County Council and Times Newspapers allowing government institutions to sue would place an undesirable fetter on freedom of the press. This was the first time that a British court had begun to develop a special privilege for the media in relation to libellous allegations made against public authorities.

5 Unintentional libel

There is a defence of unintentional libel if you can show that the words were broadcast innocently and without malice, and that an offer of amends has been made in accordance with Section 4 of the 1952 Defamation Act.

A live interviewee may make a libellous statement which the station broadcast unintentionally, but the third requirement of this defence means that an offer of amends must have been made 'as soon as practicable' (a case in 1956 decided that seven weeks later was not as soon as practicable – it would need to be more like seven days) and must not have been withdrawn. Amends can be a correction and apology and/or a payment.

To succeed in a defence of unintentional libel, you must prove that:

- The station did not know of any circumstances in which it could have understood the words to refer to the complainant, or any reason why innocent-sounding words could be defamatory (which could be tricky); and
- All reasonable care was exercised before the broadcast.

The defence of unintentional libel was introduced into the 1952 Act after the *Express* ran a short story about 'Harold Newstead, a 30-year-old Camberwell man' being convicted of bigamy, and was sued successfully by a different Harold Newstead who worked in Camberwell and had not been convicted of bigamy. However, it is debatable whether the *Express* could have satisfied the 'reasonable care' element since their story was so brief that the second Harold Newstead might still have had grounds for suing.

It is also worth considering the famous case of Artemus Jones in 1909. A reporter covering a motor festival in Dieppe invented a character called Artemus Jones in order to give colour to the story he was writing for the *Sunday Chronicle*. The invented Artemus was described as being 'with a lady who is not his wife, who must be, you know the other thing!' The paper was sued by a real Artemus Jones, a London barrister, who won substantial damages. A defence of unintentional libel might have succeeded, although the case had complicating factors, among them the fact that the real Artemus was occasionally commissioned to write law reports for the same paper, so it would not have been unreasonable for the reporter to be familiar with his name.

Although circumstances have changed since then, the dangers of inventing characters still exist.

Because of the strict provisions of this defence and the need for a quick response from the station, any unintentional libel needs legal advice – and fast!

Precedents to this defence are few, but it is an obvious candidate for settling out of court.

Phone-in programmes and 'innocent dissemination'

The most dangerous forum for the independent radio broadcaster is the live phone-in programme and much is required of producers and on-air presenters to protect their stations from the ravages of mitigation. Producers and phone operators must not allow a caller to go to air with contentious and controversial attitudes which are likely to be expressed in a defamatory fashion.

The 1996 Defamation Act has extended the scope of the innocent dissemination defence. Although it has not been tested with any precedent at the time of writing, it is possible that a radio station broadcasting an inadvertent phone-in libel might have a defence. Broadcasters of live programmes who have no effective control over the maker of the statement complained of and providers of Internet services, who again have no control, would have to show that reasonable care had been taken in the production of the programme.

Damages

The basic rule juries are given for deciding what amount of damages to award is that they should compensate the plaintiff, not punish the defendant, but the amount should be large enough to allow the plaintiff to be able to show that the 'stain' has been removed.

Exemplary or punitive damages (which means awarding a lot of money) should be awarded only in cases of unconstitutional action by a government official or where it has been shown that the defendant calculated that the advantage to himself would outweigh the compensation he would have to pay.

There is a lot of discussion about how damages are awarded, because juries can be given so little guidance on what is a reasonable amount. In other areas of the law there are guidelines as to what is considered reasonable compensation; in personal injury cases, for instance, judges are given a range of costs within which an award is considered appropriate, depending on the type of injury. This system provides more consistency in the size of awards. In libel, however, judges are not allowed to give a jury any advice on the scale of damages that might be appropriate. Given that the jury are sitting in judgment for the first time, that means they have no yardstick against which to measure their decision except what they may vaguely remember of previous cases.

At the end of 1989 a new record of £1.5 million was awarded to the former deputy chairman of the Conservative Party, Lord Aldington, for allegations by Count Nikolai Tolstoy and Nigel Watts that he was responsible for the deaths of thousands of Cossacks and Yugoslavs at the end of the Second World War. The award was for the pamphlet version of the libel; the book version was settled out of court for £30,000. In 1995, Count Tolstoy mounted a successful action at the European Court of Human Rights that the record award of damages which also included a direction to pay £1 million in costs violated his right to freedom of expression.

The English and Welsh Court of Appeal acquired the power to vary jury awards in 1990. In future libel actions, judge and lawyers could refer to the level of awards in personal injury cases.

Criminal libel

The law does not apply to live broadcasts not based on scripts. Since the risk of allegations being criminally libellous is greater within phone-in programmes, this is a very useful loophole. Prosecutions are only possible with leave of a High Court Judge. There is the idea that uttering the libel could cause a breach of the peace. It is not necessary for the plaintiff to prove that a breach of the peace would be provoked.

Malicious falsehood

This is an area of defamation law where the plaintiff can obtain legal aid. There are more actions being launched and it is essential that working independent radio journalists have an understanding of the risks. The most important point to realise is that malicious falsehood gives people the opportunity to sue for the publication of information which is untrue rather than being defamatory at the same time. The information has to be published maliciously and it has to be shown that special damage, usually financial and economic, has been caused as a result of the publication. The other essential differences to libel are that jury trial is not possible, and an action can be brought by the plaintiff's personal representatives after the plaintiff's death.

Recent cases include a former maid to the Princess Royal who in 1993 obtained legal aid and sued the *Today* newspaper for an allegation that she had stolen her employer's private letters and sold them to another newspaper. Malice was recognised because Appeal Court judges believed that a failure to check and verify police suspicions showed a reckless indifference for truth and accuracy.

Scottish libel law

The libel laws in Scotland are very similar to those in England and Wales. Justification in Scottish law is known as veritas. Scottish law has a defence called Rixa where words uttered in the heat of an argument cannot be sued over. Even if the words are defamatory they will not be actionable, but unfortunately this defence is only available to spoken communication. Fair retort is a narrow defence whereby an individual can deny charges made publicly against him. The purpose is to prevent a person being sued for saying the accuser lied. The conditions for such a broadcast have to be negotiated and prepared by a qualified Scottish media lawyer. The 1995 edition of *Scots Law for Journalists* states that the Scottish Court of Session has always recognised a 'public figure' defence.

Jury libel trials and high damages have not been as common in the Scottish Court of Session. Juries are not entitled to award exemplary damages in Scotland. Liability for damages can be mitigated where journalists publish immediate apologies. One of the most significant differences between England and Wales and Scotland is that prior restraint injunctions for defamation are very rarely permitted south of the border. The defendants usually only have to emphasise that the facts are true and that they will be able to prove them as true in any forthcoming hearing. In Scotland, injunctions are known as interdicts and the judges approach the matter with a greater willingness to grant the interdicts, sometimes with only minutes to go before broadcast transmission.

Scottish broadcast stations must lodge annual caveats with the Court of Session and local services should ensure that caveats are also lodged with the local sheriff court. The caveats will ensure that the broadcast stations as caveators will be given the chance to be heard before the interim interdict is issued.

CHAPTER 11
Contempt of court

Contempt is any act likely or calculated to obstruct the due administration of justice, i.e. anything likely to prejudice a fair trial. You can be in contempt of either a criminal court or a civil court.

Contempt of criminal courts

It is useful to think of contempt of court as divided into four bands:

1 After a crime has been committed but before there is a suspect.
2 After there is a suspect.
3 During the course of preliminary proceedings, which will usually be appearances or committal proceedings in a Magistrates Court.
4 During the course of a trial.

What can be reported and how a story can be told changes within each of the bands.

1 The first band covers the period when, theoretically, you can really run with the story. However, there is a dangerous period between when a crime is committed and when the accused actually appears in court, because you cannot always be absolutely certain where all the pieces fit in. If the police arrest someone at the scene of a crime, or during a car chase, or whatever, the contempt rules apply from the moment of arrest or warrant of arrest.

2 When the police issue an appeal for help in tracing someone for whom a warrant has been issued, it is strictly contempt to broadcast it, but there are no known cases of prosecution, and the Attorney General of the day told Parliament during the debate on the Bill stage of the Contempt Act 1981 that this was a public service and he

wanted the media to continue to assist in the apprehension of a wanted man.

But apart from the specific appeal, once a person has been arrested or charged, or a warrant issued, there is no such thing as a 'murder victim', 'robbery victim', or 'rape victim'. There are dead people or injured people, because from now on it is up to a jury to decide whether it was murder, robbery or rape. If you use such words inadvisedly, the court may decide you have affected their judgment and are therefore in contempt.

So at this stage a murder story must run along these lines: 'A man has been charged with the murder of Mrs Ada Bloggs, whose body was found in Smith Square earlier today.' You can say she had head injuries, but not that she was beaten up, or attacked, or battered. Nothing, in fact, which implies a deliberate attack.

The broad rule is that you can report the crime, but you must word your report so that it does not suggest that anyone is the culprit. So you can say a man was arrested after a post office robbery, but you cannot identify the man arrested.

You must also never describe someone who has been arrested, because that might prejudice any future defence argument contesting identity.

You must be very cautious when someone is 'helping police with their inquiries'. While it is true that the person may be there voluntarily and not charged with any offence, there is no way you can know that. In any case, if someone is there who does not want to be, in law that person has been arrested. If you name someone who is there voluntarily, you are in danger of a libel action later on. Choose your words with care – even skill.

3 Once the case gets to court, what can and can't be said is strictly specified. During preliminary proceedings, what can be reported is laid down in law, but once the case is being heard in full, reports of what the court hears can start.

The Magistrates Courts Act 1980

Under this Act, every sentence of the following story of a committal contains at least one contempt of court:

> A mother of three from Coolstown has been committed for trial on a shoplifting charge. Blonde housewife, Elsie Jones, was wearing a green trouser suit when she appeared at Peckham Green Magistrates Court. She waved at her children as she left the dock.

Contempt of court **133**

You cannot say she is a mother of three, that she is a blonde wearing a trouser suit, or that she waved at her children.

The Act lists the points you can report from preliminary hearings for offences triable by jury. You may only report:

- the name of the court and the names of the examining justices
- names addresses and occupations of parties and witnesses
- ages of defendants and witnesses
- the charges or a summary of them
- names of counsel and solicitors
- the decision of the court to commit for trial
- decisions of any defendant(s) not committed
- charges on which the defendant is committed
- court to which the defendant is committed
- date and place to which any committal is adjourned
- arrangements as to bail
- whether legal aid was granted
- any decision of the court to lift, or not to lift, these reporting restrictions.

These restrictions usually apply during appearances in a Magistrates Court when the case might end up being heard by a jury at the Crown Court, but they are in force during any proceedings before the case is heard in full. For example, the law says that people being held in custody before trial must appear before the court every seven days (unless there is agreement from all sides to amend the length of time) while a case is being prepared and before the committal begins. These are colloquially known as 'up and downs', because nothing really happens between the defendant coming up from the cells and being taken back down again. In particularly newsworthy cases a reporter might be sent to the up and down, but the restrictions apply because these appearances are part of the preliminary proceedings.

Reporting restrictions in contempt do not apply if:

- A defendant applies to have them lifted. If there is more than one defendant, the magistrates have to decide whether it is in the interests of justice to lift restrictions (unless all the defendants wish them to be lifted).
- The court decides not to commit for trial.
- The court decides to deal with one or more defendants summarily. Even if some defendants are committed, the evidence relating to those tried summarily can be reported regardless of whether it impinges on the case of those sent for trial.
- All the defendants have been tried at the Crown Court. This means that once the main case has finished, you can report evidence

134 A Guide to Commercial Radio Journalism

given at committal. It is seldom newsworthy if it was not also used in the Crown Court case, but if it is, it is treated as a contemporaneous report, and therefore privileged.

In the case of serious crimes, some cases have to go to the Crown Court. But in cases where the defendant chooses a jury trial, this is often reported even though it is not strictly among the ten permitted points. So far, at least, the courts have not stepped on this practice, because it is seen to be to the defendant's advantage.

These restrictions are heavy and make reporting of some cases very difficult, but they are designed to protect the defendant, a duty the courts take very seriously. So learn what you can report by heart and stay within the boundaries.

Even if reporting restrictions have been lifted, there are dangers of a report being contemptuous. It is obviously contempt to take sides, or imply that anybody is guilty – or innocent – of an offence. And you should never report that someone has previous convictions, even if the police say in open court that they are opposing bail because of them.

Generally, you can be in contempt if a report interferes with the course of justice:

- in a particular case, e.g. prejudicing a fair trial, or
- by obstructing the course of justice generally, or
- by failing to comply with a court order.

The Contempt of Court Act 1981

This Act codified some of the common law on contempt, and was intended to help clarify our position. It applies to both civil and criminal courts. The Act says that any contemptuous broadcast falls within the 'strict liability' rule. 'Strict' as used here means the courts will presume intent rather than the prosecution having to prove it.

If a contempt case is to succeed the following two elements must be proved:

- that the report creates a substantial risk of serious impediment or prejudice to particular proceedings, and
- that those proceedings are active.

Proceedings being active
Proceedings are deemed as being active in criminal proceedings:

- When an arrest is made without warrant.

- On the issue of a warrant for arrest.
- On the issue of a summons.
- On an indictment being served, or any document specifying charges.
- On oral charging.
- If an inquest has been opened.
- If it is an appeal, when an application to appeal or an application for leave to appeal is made.

Proceedings are active in civil courts when the case is 'set down' in the High Court, i.e. when a case goes onto the waiting list to be heard or a date is set.

In inquests and tribunals proceedings become active when a date for the hearing is fixed.

Proceedings in criminal cases cease to be active when:

- The arrested person is released without charge.
- No arrest is made within a year of the issue of a warrant, although warrants can be renewed.
- The case is discontinued.
- The defendant is acquitted or sentenced.
- The defendant is found unfit to be tried, unfit to plead, or the court orders the charge to lie on file.

In civil proceedings, a case remains active until it is disposed of, abandoned, or withdrawn.

Recordings of proceedings

Recordings cannot be made in any court unless the permission of the justice has been given in advance. Even if recording is allowed (which is rare, even though practice directions say judges should accede to such a request; more often sound recorders are physically taken away from journalists), no part of the recording can be used on air. If a recording is made, it can only be used to check accuracy. Broadcasting any part of the proceedings is contempt.

It is a subject of debate whether court proceedings should be open to the television cameras, as is the case in many other countries. This is of particular interest to radio, because many of the reservations voiced about television do not apply. The existence of microphones need not intimidate witnesses, and radio cannot accidentally reveal the identity of jurors. As far as editing is concerned, written or voiced reports are already subject to editing, so why should recorded extracts be treated any differently?

During the course of a court case

Criminal courts

Once the magistrates or a jury are actually hearing the case, life becomes more tolerable. But the basic rules of contempt still apply. You must not broadcast anything which could be seen to prejudice the trial. In addition, you must leave out anything that happens when the jury is not in the court room, anything the judge directs the jury to ignore, and anything which indicates a previous conviction unless it is mentioned by the defence, in the court room, while the jury is present. Juries are sometimes sent out of the court room, for instance while submissions are made (such as 'no case to answer') or if there are arguments about the admissibility of evidence. The reason they are taken out of the court room is so that they are not swayed by what is taking place, and you will be in clear contempt of court if you report what happens in their absence. Border Television was found in contempt when it reported the guilty pleas of a defendant in a criminal trial who pleaded guilty to certain charges when the jury were not there, but who then went on to contest others.

The courts also have the power, under Section 4 of the Contempt of Court Act 1981, to order that the reporting of some matters should be delayed. In such cases the eventual report will be considered contemporaneous and therefore privileged when it does come out. But if a Section 4 order is made unfairly you can opt for judicial review under the Criminal Justice Act 1988, if you and/or the station can afford the legal fees.

There are occasions when someone has been found guilty by the jury but there is a delay before the judge passes sentence. This always sparks off debates in the newsroom. Strictly speaking, the Act says restrictions apply until sentence, but some judges take the view that it is the jury who need protecting from undue influence, and they are not likely to be swayed by mere media background coverage or reports. Not all judges take that view, however, so unless you know a particular judge's attitude, be sure that a report has been cleared by management before you run it.

When a case ends, a defence lawyer may say that there are plans to appeal against conviction or sentence, but the law of contempt does not apply until the appeal is actually lodged, so there is, in the words of Lord Havers, the Attorney General of the day, a 'free for all' time. Once sentence has been passed, we can run reports or background interviews until the leave to appeal has been submitted, which usually takes days rather than hours.

Civil courts

Most civil cases are heard by judges sitting alone, without juries, and the law worries about the effect media reports might have on juries and lay magistrates much more than on judges. The courts have ruled that judges are trained to consider only the evidence before them and not be unduly influenced by outside events, so any contemptuous statement would need to be particularly severe before proceedings were instigated.

The danger of contempt will be greater, however, if it is a case in which a judge is sitting with lay people, which occurs in some sorts of appeals.

Court of appeal

Judges sitting in the Court of Appeal (and the House of Lords) are deemed to be above any potential influence by journalists, so contempt would only apply if it fell within the category of 'scandalising the courts'.

Defences to contempt of court

Under Section 3 of the Act, there is a defence in **not knowing proceedings were active**. To be able to claim this defence, though, you have to prove that you took 'all reasonable care' in establishing that you did not know and had no reason to suspect that proceedings were active. If a story smacks of possible proceedings, you need to check with the police to make sure there is no suspect. To cover yourself, make a note of the time and the name of the police officer or official you spoke to.

Discussion of public affairs

As a result of the *Sunday Times*/Distillers tangle over the drug thalidomide in 1974, Section 5 of the Act was introduced so that a discussion in good faith of public affairs would not be treated as contempt if the risk of prejudice to a particular trial was incidental to the discussion.

Substantial risk

As Lord Lane said in defining 'substantial risk of serious prejudice', 'a slight or trivial risk of serious prejudice is not enough, nor is a substantial risk of slight prejudice'. An illustrative example is that of Paul

Magee, an IRA terrorist and murderer. Paul Magee shot dead a part-time special police constable in North Yorkshire who had challenged his car on a remote country road. Magee became a fugitive on the run before being arrested while hiding in a ditch. After his arrest Independent Television News named the arrested man as Paul Magee and stated that he was a convicted IRA terrorist who had escaped from the Maze prison in Belfast while serving life imprisonment for the murder of an SAS officer. The following day the *Daily Mail*, *Daily Express*, *Today* and *Northern Echo* (published in Darlington) newspapers published similar material. Since Mr Magee was due to stand trial for murder and other terrorist related offences, it is hard to imagine a more prejudicial publication. But the test of 'substantial risk' was raised vigorously by the lawyers representing the news organisations being prosecuted for contempt. They had on their side the fact that the trial was to take place 9 months later. The *Northern Echo* had the advantage that only 146 copies of its paper were on sale in London where the trial for murder and attempted murder would be staged at the Old Bailey. All the organisations were acquitted by the Divisional Court. The time lapse was considered sufficient to undermine the threshold required for 'a substantial risk'. The *Northern Echo*'s restricted publication to the North of England also offered protection.

Note that if you intend to impede or prejudice justice by your action, or if you are 'reckless' in the sense of not thinking or caring about the result of your action, this defence does not exist.

Common law contempt

Most prosecutions these days are brought under the Contempt of Court Act. The old common law of contempt was unheard of between 1981, when the Act came into force, and 1987, when it was resurrected during the Spycatcher case.

Under common law contempt, there is no test of whether proceedings are active, only that they are 'pending' or 'imminent', but intent does have to be proved. The law is vague and makes journalists' jobs difficult, because reporters and editors have to pre-judge a court's decision on the imminence of a case. The 1981 Act was, therefore, greeted with considerable relief. In 1987, however, all the inherent difficulties reappeared.

Intent

In the *Guardian* and *Observer* appeals in the Spycatcher case, Sir John Donaldson, Master of the Rolls, said that when there was conduct 'intended to impede or prejudice the administration of justice ... intent need not be expressly avowed or admitted, but can be inferred from all the circumstances'. Since 'intent' in law means having regard to the natural consequences of actions, he was saying that being reckless with the consequences is equivalent to intent.

Imminence

In 1988 the *Sun* was fined as a result of its campaign to imprison a doctor for the alleged rape of an eight-year-old. No proceedings had begun, but Lord Justice Watkins said proceedings were 'imminent' because a prosecution was virtually certain to be started 'in the near future'. He also said that the editor had become convinced of the doctor's guilt and tried to persuade *Sun* readers to a similar view: 'That is trial by newspaper, a form of activity which strikes directly at a jury's impartiality.'

In deciding that case, the court relied in part on a 1903 case which said it was not so much that the case had begun, more that it had not finished. The 'imminence' of proceedings is vague and uncertain, but the courts will decide on its application depending on all the circumstances of each case.

The *Sun* was fined £75,000 and an application to appeal to the House of Lords was refused.

Even though common law contempt is seldom used now, remember it if you are covering a breaking story. If it is the sort of story that is likely to end up in front of a jury, be mindful of any prejudicial ingredients.

Scandalising the courts

The courts have decided that conduct of judges and decisions of the court are matters of legitimate public concern and debate. However, we must never impute improper motives to anyone involved in the administration of justice, and abuse of a judge or attacks on the integrity or impartiality of a judge or court is prohibited. It is years since anyone has been prosecuted for scandalising the courts. Lord Salmon has said: 'No criticism of a judgment, however vigorous, can amount to contempt of court if it keeps within the limits of reasonable courtesy and of good faith. Do not be cowed by the laws of libel and contempt. As we have seen, the law gives you some protection in both areas. Find a sensible balance between what you know is beyond the pale and self-censorship.'

Good faith

Section 5 of the 1981 Contempt of Court Act states:

> A publication made as or as part of a discussion in good faith of public affairs or other matters of general public interest is not to be treated as a contempt of court under the strict liability rule if the risk of impairment or prejudice to particular legal proceedings is merely incidental to the discussion.

Interviewing jurors

The 1981 Contempt of Court Act created a new contempt offence – interviewing jurors. This does not stop the media interviewing jurors about what it was like to be a juror, ask their opinion of the trial or anything else as long as nothing is solicited concerning the deliberations process. The *Mail On Sunday* published an article headlined 'Common people ... Common sense ... Common justice' and described conversations between jury members during the Blue Arrow fraud trial. Opinions about the evidence and the disclosure that one jury member only agreed with the others because he wanted to go home were also included. At the Divisional Court fines totalling £60,000 were imposed on newspaper, editor and journalist.

The Scottish criminal justice system

Although the same piece of legislation concerning contempt of court (the 1981 Contempt of Court Act) applies both north and south of the border, the Scottish judges interpret contempt much more strictly and severely. You must also be very careful if you work for radio stations whose catchment areas straddle the border. At this stage simply accept the principle that in Scotland you should only report the bare facts of a court appearance at the beginning of the criminal justice process and that any reference at all to associated information, even non-contentious facts, will be regarded as contempt.

In 1979 a man called Stuurman, his wife and two others were arrested in Scotland and charged with drugs offences. A press briefing from the investigating authorities in England alleged they were members of an international drugs running gang and had been the target of an Interpol hunt for many years. Radio Forth broadcast the report which emanated from the national bulletin prepared in London by IRN and were fined £10,000 for contempt.

CHAPTER 12
Restrictions on reporting

Election law

Election campaigns are full of interest and good copy, but they are also a source of serious headaches. Newspapers do not operate under the same restrictions as TV and radio during the run-up to elections. Newspapers can endorse particular party lines, run stories in accordance with the paper's viewpoint, and carry election stories and results of their opinion polls on polling day itself. No such leniency for us.

The Broadcasting Acts 1981 and 1990 and the Representation of the People Act 1983 (RPA), combine to demand that the broadcast media show no prejudice or bias. We not only have to ensure fair and balanced election coverage, we also have to be able to show that we have done so.

Under the Broadcasting Act, we are under a general requirement to ensure that 'due impartiality is preserved on the part of the persons providing the programmes in respect of political or industrial controversy or relating to current public policy'. During the run-up to an election, that requirement takes on even more weight.

Pending periods

Elections can be divided into four main time bands:

- Pending before nominations have closed but after an election date has been announced. It is most unwise to interview or report on the activities of any candidate during this period because it is not possible to identify all the potential candidates.
- Pending after nominations have closed. All the candidates are known, and discussions and constituency reports can begin.

- Eve of poll. No discussion programmes can be aired about election issues, but balanced constituency reports or news wraps can be.
- Polling day. No interviews with candidates, no reports at all except straight facts about the weather, the rate of turnout, arrangements for counting, expected time of declaration, etc. You are allowed to give factual reports of opinion polls as long as they have not been commissioned by your station.

When the first pending period begins varies according to what sort of election it is.

- National elections: from the date at which the intention to dissolve Parliament is announced by the Queen.
- Parliamentary by-elections: from the date the writ is issued, usually in Parliament.
- Local elections: from 5 weeks before election day.
- Local by-elections: from the date of publishing the notice of election.
- European elections: from 5 weeks before election day.
- Scottish Parliament and Welsh Assembly elections: from 5 weeks before election day.

The pending period for any election (and therefore the lifting of restrictions) only ends with the close of polls on polling day.

Balanced and equal time allocations

During an election period, we have to present election coverage in one of two ways, depending on what sort of coverage it is. 'Balanced time' in the context of the RPA means a percentage of time allocated to each party, whereas 'equal time' means exactly what it says.

Balanced time applies whenever a candidate is talking about constituency issues, or 'enhancing their standing', i.e. saying why people should vote for a particular candidate. Equal time applies whenever party policy is being discussed.

Balanced time

The amount of time allotted to each party in a local election is a matter of editorial judgment, taking national and local circumstances into account, and the station management will advise you on the percentages. In a national election the balance is determined by the Radio Authority and again you will be advised of the percentages. You do not have to make these calculations for yourself, but you must adhere to them carefully.

The percentages will usually be based on the votes cast in the last comparable election and the number of candidates standing for a particular party. A hiccup occurred in the system in the 1979 general election when the SDP was a new party; a special configuration was adopted, based on the number of members they had, their standing in the polls, and so on.

Balanced time not only covers a percentage of time, but the time of day as well. For example, a broadcast featuring one party in the morning drive-time programme cannot be 'balanced' by giving another party their proportion of time in a programme going out at 21.00 because of the difference in the size of the audience. Even within individual programmes, it is good practice to run a series of election reports at about the same time within the programme.

The balanced percentages you are given could look something like this: Labour 35%; Conservatives 30%; Liberal Democrats 20%; all others 15% ('all others' can mount up – it is not unusual for there to be eight or more candidates in a constituency). By polling day, the station must be able to show that it has given each party its correct overall percentage of air time. This is done by keeping election logs.

Some programmes or stations find it easier to restrict their election coverage to balanced wraps so that they know they are always on course. That means that within, say, a 5-minute report each party has the right percentage of air time: in our example, Labour would get 2 minute 15 seconds, Conservative would have 1 minute 30 seconds, the Liberal Democrats 1 minute, and the others 45 seconds. 'All others' is covered by that bit of the report when you hear the broadcaster saying 'And there are six other candidates running in the constituency. They are ...' Since those six have only 45 seconds between them, they are each allowed about 7 seconds, so giving their name and party fulfils their time allocation.

If you are putting together a wrap or offering balanced time, all the candidates of parties allocated a percentage must take part or give you written permission to carry on without them. This requirement created real problems during the general elections of the 1970s. The National Front had been apportioned a percentage of time, and therefore had to be included in any constituency report where they had a candidate. The Labour Party made a policy decision not to 'appear on the same platform' as an NF member, which included media coverage. This meant that the broadcast media were confined to compiling constituency reports in only those areas where no one from the NF was standing.

Balanced wraps are a neat way of maintaining balanced time in news programmes or bulletins, but obviously are not possible in phone-ins.

Equal time

If you invite parties to send in representative candidates to make policy statements, they must be given equal time. It is usually easier to organise equal time contributions as a series of programmes; keeping candidates to equal time within a programme can get very difficult as they all try to pick up on each other's statements. But it is unwise to go ahead with the first programme until you have arranged dates for all the participants.

There is an additional problem in deciding which parties to include. The RPA does not necessarily expect you to give equal time to all the 'fringe' parties, but you should consult your management before deciding on a cut-off point.

Candidates

In the period before nominations close, the RPA restrictions apply to any self-declared or provisional candidate or any person who on common-sense grounds could be regarded as a potential or likely candidate. That is why it is unwise to interview anyone in the pending period before nominations close. Once the nominations have closed, you have the full list of candidates and therefore know whom to include.

Remember, a candidate cannot take part in any programme or report which relates to the election or election issues, or which may 'enhance their general standing' unless either (1) all the candidates take part and are given balanced time, or (2) those candidates not taking part give their written consent and a balanced report of the activity of those not taking part is included in the programme.

If, say, the three main candidates are each taking part in turn in a programme on successive days, you need the written consent of all the other candidates for each day's programme.

A candidate may also be a party's spokesperson on, say, housing, transport or education, either locally or nationally. As part of your normal news coverage, the spokesperson is allowed to take part outside the normal rules of balance. This can only happen when such a spokesperson is dealing with a matter that has total news justification and is not merely enhancing a party's standing. If in doubt, ask your editor or management. However, comments must be restricted to broad policy and must not refer to particular matters in a particular constituency. The contributor should be introduced as 'the spokesman on ...' and no mention should be made of his own candidacy or constituency.

Government continues to operate during an election, but the constitutional issues can become very complex. If possible, when you have any doubts, check with your management before broadcasting anything. If for some reason that is not possible, presume it is part of the balance, and note it for logging purposes until you can check. Remember that even Prime Ministers are candidates and should not be allowed to make comments on their constituencies or enhance their parties' standing.

News not related to the election can be reported. For example, if a candidate is in a car accident or has won the pools, that can be reported as long as that person's candidacy is not part of the report. Again, be careful, as some news might be seen to enhance (or undermine) a candidate's reputation.

Phone-ins

A candidate must never be allowed on air as a caller, and no candidate or potential candidate should be invited to take part in a phone-in until after nominations have closed.

If a candidate takes part as a guest, then all candidates must take part. In a local election, if candidates take part individually, on separate days, then each candidate must give written consent for the others to take part on the days when they are not there.

Callers should only be allowed to comment on individual candidates when that candidate is in the studio and able to make an immediate reply.

As with general news or wraps, the time allotted to candidates or parties must be balanced, unless the programme is about policy, in which case the equal time rule applies. The complications of getting the balance right mean that it is easier and safer to stick to discussions of policies on phone-ins.

If you have a series of phone-ins on policy matters, the whole of the time the spokesperson for the party is on air is considered to be of benefit to that party. Therefore, if someone from the Labour Party appears on an hour-long phone-in, it does not matter if most of the calls are from anti-Labour people. Since the person is there to answer on behalf of the Party, it is treated as favourable to them and the whole hour is logged as pro-Labour.

General calls put to air must be balanced according to the percentages appropriate for the election or, more probably, comply with equal time if the call is about party policy. That means making a note on the election log which includes the caller's first name, how long they spoke on air and which party benefited. This can be another real headache, for callers sometimes ring to say why they are not going to vote for a particular party without speaking on behalf of any other. In such cases, it is best to note down, e.g., 'Sam of Peckham, 3 minutes, anti-Labour' in the hope that other callers will ring to put down the other parties so that in the end they cancel each other out.

News programmes

The same basic rules about the appearance of candidates and balance apply to news bulletins and magazines. Full logs of all election coverage in bulletins should be kept by each newsdesk, unless the bulletin comes from IRN, in which case they will keep track of their coverage balance. Local bulletin coverage must be logged and balanced.

Extracts of speeches by local candidates about local issues cannot be used in either bulletins or programmes unless all the candidates are used according to the balance percentages.

Logs

In order to deal with complaints as well as to be able to show that you have kept within the Broadcasting Acts and the RPA, full records must be kept. They must show the name of the programme, date, time and duration of election material broadcast (whether live or recorded), names of participants and the parties represented. In phone-ins, the number of callers favouring each party and the length of time each spoke on air must be noted.

Balanced wraps should be listed as such with their transmission date, time and duration. It is good practice to keep the scripts of all wraps in order to refer back if there are any questions.

Most station managers leave blank logs with each producer or editor so that each programme or news area is responsible for maintaining the correct balance, with the logs finding their way back to management each week or so for a running check to be sure coverage is on course.

The next time polling stations close and an election is over listen and you will hear the collective sigh of relief from the broadcast media. The kid gloves are back where they belong, and we can get down to covering political issues in the time-honoured way. It may be a compliment of sorts for the law-makers to believe that TV and radio have such a strong influence on the voters, but by the time the polls close, you will be hurling yourself headlong into covering the results and finally talking to one or two candidates without worrying about percentages, balance and fairness.

Formal orders restricting reporting

Magistrates and Crown Courts are now obliged to keep proper records and issue proper notices regarding orders made under the 1981 Contempt of Court Act and Children and Young Persons Acts. An official of the court should be able to give you a copy or read it out in detail. When you seek the information make a note of the time and the name of the person you spoke to. Even better, record the conversation so you have an independently verifiable electronic record. You have to bear in mind that the onus is on you to find out the nature of the order.

Postponement of trials

Two types of order are imposed under the Contempt of Court Act 1981. They are known as Section 4(2) and Section 11 orders. Section 4(2) orders are imposed to postpone reporting of parts or the whole of trials. The purpose is to avoid 'a substantial risk of prejudice to the administration of justice' in future cases, or in the trial taking place. Most orders are made to cover 'trials within a trial'. These are occasions when the jury is sent out, so it is common sense that matters being discussed could be potentially prejudicial.

Other Section 4(2) orders are made where an indictment containing a series of charges against one or more defendants has been split. This means there will be a series of trials running consecutive to one another. Judges should make orders that enable as much fair and accurate reporting as is necessary.

Anonymity

Section 11 orders are prohibitive for all time and are designed to give anonymity to individuals giving evidence where the Common Law allows it in terms of previous precedent. In 1974 a Divisional Court case sanctioned anonymity for blackmail witnesses who would not go to the police if a public trial revealed the very information which was the source of the blackmailer's threat. Since 1981 judges have begun making Section 11 orders for witnesses who are embarrassed or fear potential or real intimidation as a result of giving evidence.

Protection of officials

These orders are also being made to protect police, customs officers, MI5 and MI6 officers who wish to continue working under cover and who fear revenge attacks. A woman police constable who worked under cover to befriend a man accused of murdering Rachel Nickell on Wimbledon Common was protected in this way even though the trial judge condemned the *agent provocateur* style of investigation. The Section 11 order can only be valid if the identity of the witness is withheld from the public before the court.

Rape and other sexual offences

The Sexual Offences (Amendment) Act 1976 has been further amended by the Criminal Justice Act 1988 so that a woman's identity is protected from the moment it is alleged she has been the victim of a rape offence, and that protection lasts for the whole of her lifetime. Her name can only be broadcast if she gives her written consent.

In August 1996 Ralston Edwards subjected his rape complainant to a six day ordeal of cross-examination. He was representing himself and wearing the same clothes he wore on the day of the alleged attack. The victim, Mrs Julia Mason, decided to waive her anonymity after the guilty verdict and sentencing because she believed that no sexual offence complainant should undergo such an experience again.

The Criminal Justice and Public Order Act 1994 extended the anonymity to include complainants of male rape. These restrictions apply in any proceedings for rape; attempted rape; aiding, abetting, counselling and procuring rape or attempted rape; incitement to rape; conspiracy to rape; and burglary with intent to rape.

Apart from giving her or his written permission, the complainant can be named only if:

- the accused satisfies a Crown Court judge before the trial starts that lifting the restriction is necessary to induce witnesses to come forward and his defence will be prejudiced otherwise; or
- the judge decides that anonymity puts an unreasonable and serious restriction on reporting the trial and that it should be lifted in the public interest.

Note that you still cannot name the complainant if the man is acquitted!

Until the 1988 Criminal Justice Act came into effect, the accused could not be named unless he was convicted. Now, however, the identity of the accused is no longer protected in law.

The restrictions on naming the rape victim do not apply if rape is merely mentioned in another trial when there are no proceedings going ahead on a rape charge or on any charge other than those listed above, e.g. indecent assault. The name ban can be lifted if the judge consents to a request from an editor or journalist; the request is often granted, for example, in cases in which the defendant faces a charge of murder as well as rape.

Sometimes a patchwork identification can be achieved because some reports give certain details, others different ones. The Press Council has therefore suggested that reporters and editors co-operate with one another and agree which details should come out.

The Sexual Offences Amendment Act 1992

Anonymity was extended to the complainants of other sexual offences from 1 August 1992. Where a person is accused of buggery, indecent conduct towards a child, and a range of other sexual offences, it became an offence to publish any matter likely to lead members of the public to identify someone against whom the offence is alleged to have been committed during the victim's lifetime.

Rehabilitation of Offenders Act 1974

This Act was passed to enable someone who has been convicted of a relatively minor offence to live it down and be protected from having the conviction dragged up from the far distant past. How much time must elapse before a conviction becomes 'spent', and therefore not suitable for reporting, depends on how long a sentence was originally passed.

Any sentence which imprisoned someone for more than 30 months can never be spent. If a person was sentenced for between 6 and 30 months, the conviction is not spent for 10 years, and sentences involving less than 6 months take 7 years before being spent. If no prison sentence was imposed, the rehabilitation period is 5 years, unless the court decided on an absolute discharge, which carries a 6-month period.

Generally speaking, it is not ethical to report spent convictions, but so far there have not been any cases of papers or stations being sued when they have done so in genuine 'public interest'.

Children and young persons

The law defines children as being between 10 and 14, and young persons as between 14 and 17. Both are usually dealt with by juvenile courts. Children under 10 are deemed incapable of criminal acts.

The right of reporters to attend juvenile courts is one of the rare occasions when we have a special right which is not afforded to the public at large. However, no report of juvenile proceedings can reveal the name, address, school or any other particulars that would identify any juvenile involved in any way, whether the juvenile is the object of the hearing or a witness. Further, any adult court can prohibit the reporting of any material leading to the identification of juveniles involved in any proceedings before it.

Juvenile courts were established under the Children and Young Persons Act 1933, and their powers have been altered by subsequent Acts. The Children and Young Persons Act 1969 says that the court or the Home Secretary can lift the ban on identifying a person under the age of 17 only in the interests of avoiding injustice to the juvenile. The Crime (Sentences) Act 1997 has amended the 1933 Act so that the magistrates can lift the restriction to permit identification of convicted youths when it is in the public interest.

The law is very serious about protecting children and young people from the gaze and possible censure of the public, so be sure you adhere to the regulations.

Appeals from the juvenile court go to a Crown Court, or High Court, but the restrictions on revealing the identity of the juvenile still apply. A young person can also be sent for trial by jury at a Crown Court if the sentence for the offence is sufficiently serious to be punishable by 14 or more years' imprisonment, such as homicide, robbery or rape.

Juvenile courts deal with more than just crime. They also take action in cases where children (even below the age of 10) are in need of special care. They have the power to take children from their parents and put them into care, they can order special supervision, or require parents to mend their ways and take better care of a child. In cases of mental illness, they can send children to hospital or appoint special guardians.

Preliminary and pre-trial hearings

In preliminary hearings in fraud and sexual offence cases, and pre-trial hearings at the Crown Court in England and Wales, statutory reporting restrictions apply and can catch out an unwary newsroom. Sometimes serious and complex fraud cases are transferred under the 1987 Criminal Justice Act from Magistrates Courts to the Crown Court without the usual committal for trial. Hearings take place where the accused applies for the prosecution to be struck out on the grounds of insufficient evidence. The 1996 Criminal Procedures and Investigations Act imposes reporting restrictions on hearings held to try to clarify the issues that will have to be decided by the jurors and to save time.

The 1991 Criminal Justice Act allows for a process of speeding up proceedings against people charged with serious sexual offences against children. The case is transferred to the Crown Court and the defendants are entitled to make applications for the case to be discharged. The same type of restrictions apply. If the application is successful the restrictions are lifted. If unsuccessful, they remain in force.

Domestic proceedings and family law cases

Reports of divorce proceedings and other matters relating to family law have the following restrictions:

- Names, addresses and occupations of parties and witnesses.
- A concise statement of the charges, defence and counter-charges in support of which evidence is given or (in the case of a declaration of status) the declaration sought,.
- Submissions on points of law and rulings of the court.
- The judgment of the court and observations by the judge.

The ability to report these hearings depends on whether they are open to the public. It has to be remembered that the charges and counter-charges can only be reported if evidence has been given to support them. Domestic proceedings can be heard in the Magistrate, County and High Courts. Most of the cases in the Family Division of the High Court are heard behind closed doors. The 1989 Children Act introduced restrictions to protect the identity of children in care proceedings. Nothing can be reported which includes material which is intended or likely to identify the child, or the child's school. A child under this legislation is 'a person under the age of 18'. Magistrates now have the discretionary power to exclude the press and public from care proceedings.

All the parties must be anonymous in adoption hearings, charges and counter-charges cannot be summarised and nothing must be published which could identify the child.

The press and public have no access to wardship proceedings and it is a contempt of court to publish any information relating to wardship proceedings.

In child abuse scandals, the courts have indicated that the public interest in reporting certain issues should allow the naming of a local authority and publication of interviews as long as the anonymity of the children involved is maintained.

New legislative restrictions, 1993-96

Industrial tribunals acquired banning powers in the Trade Union Reform and Employment Rights Act 1993 and Disability Discrimination Act 1995. Sexual harassment at work became a significant social issue in the 1990s but actions by people complaining of misconduct can now be covered by reporting bans on the identity of the complainant. The logical outcome of such a ban is that it is usually impossible to identify the alleged offender and the organisation he or she works for.

The 1995 legislation provided a right to tackle employers accused of discriminating against people on the basis of their disabilities. However, the reporting ban powers preventing identification of individuals who advance evidence of a medical or intimate nature which 'might cause significant embarrassment' are more than likely to lead to a reluctance to report such cases.

The 1996 Criminal Procedure and Investigations Act introduced a new court reporting restriction in relation to allegations against third parties during pleas of mitigation. The restriction power lasts for one year which is long enough to disable the news and current affairs interest in any comments made during the mitigation speech. The purpose of this law was to protect innocent people stigmatised and blamed by convicted defendants through their lawyers' mitigation speeches.

The few civil actions determined by juries are also susceptible to prejudicial reporting. *Private Eye* magazine was held to be in contempt for publications prior to a High Court libel case. News organisations must bear in mind that they can be held in contempt of inquests conducted by coroners in England and Wales. The equivalent Fatal Accident Enquiries in Scotland are also protected against broadcasts which create a substantial risk of serious prejudice. Many coroners' inquests in England and Wales are decided by 11 person juries.

The Prevention of Terrorism (Temporary Provisions) Act 1989

This act makes it a criminal offence to possess information which a person knows or believes might be of material assistance in

- preventing the commission by any other person of an act of terrorism connected with the affairs of Northern Ireland: or
- in securing the apprehension, prosecution or conviction of any other person for an offence involving the commission, preparation or instigation of such an act.

This offence carries a maximum sentence of five years' imprisonment. In 1994 Channel 4 and the independent production company Box Productions were fined £75,000 for failing to disclose the identity of the source in a controversial programme making allegations against the RUC.

Unlike the Police and Criminal Evidence Act which requires that journalists are given seven days' notice, no notice is required under the terrorism legislation. The 1989 Official Secrets Act also provides powers to demand disclosure of sources over the leaking of confidential and classified government information. There are other pieces of legislation which give government officials and investigating bodies the power to insist on disclosure. The police, customs and excise, and the security services have powers of surveillance and monitoring which can compromise journalistic independence and protection of sources.

The Official Secrets Act 1989

Under this act the prosecution has to prove that the information disclosed by a journalist was damaging and the journalist knew or had reasonable cause to believe that it would be damaging. There is no public interest defence.

Freedom of Information Bill

At the time of writing, the government has published a White Paper which paves the way for a Freedom of Information Bill in the next Parliament. If enacted, people in the United Kingdom would have a legal right to see information held by almost every public organisation in the country. Government departments, armed forces, police authorities, National Health Service trusts, local authorities, privatised utilities and public service broadcasters would have to open their records to examination. A powerful new Information Commissioner would be appointed and he/she would have strong powers to compel the provision of records. Intelligence and national security bodies would still be exempted from the provisions of the act, but at this stage the UK legislation promises to be more powerful than similar laws abroad. The White Paper states that under most exceptions, only information capable of causing 'substantial damage' could be withheld. Most overseas exceptions refer to 'damage', 'harm' or 'injury' but do not require the damage to be substantial.

Breach of copyright

The law of copyright is at least as complex as that of defamation, but most of the pitfalls will be avoided by an agreed payment of royalties or at least the implied agreement of an author who wants publicity knowing that you represent a radio station and that you are recording. But the dangers of infringing copyright remain, and what follows is no more than a very brief guide. If there is any question in your mind, get advice before anything which could be copyrighted goes out on air.

Copyright in broadcast material is held by the RA or the BBC, and in the case of ILR that copyright is then transferred to an individual station by its licence from the RA. ILR stations cannot use recordings of BBC broadcasts without the BBC's permission (and usually a credit) and vice versa. If one of the authorities (i.e. the RA or BBC) has obtained the exclusive right to a programme or event, the other will be in breach of copyright if a broadcast impinges on that exclusivity. For example, for the time being the BBC has an exclusive agreement for broadcasting commentaries from the All England Lawn Tennis Wimbledon fortnight, while ILR is given what is called 'news access'. That means we can report what is happening (as long as it does not exceed 2 minutes per hour), but we cannot offer live, blow-by-blow descriptions of a match.

The Copyright Act 1988, which came into force in the second half of 1989, has replaced the old and much criticised Act of 1956. It is intended to make the law clearer and easier to follow; whether it succeeds remains to be seen.

The principle of copyright is to give the 'author' of a piece the right to prevent others reproducing the work without permission. Under the new Act, however, this does not apply to employees of a radio station. The law says that the station is the 'first owner' of staff journalists' material. Freelancers, on the other hand, still hold copyright in their pieces. In principle, therefore, the station needs to get the freelancer's agreement before an item can be passed on for use by some other broadcasting outlet.

The law protects the physical thing, not the idea, so that if, for instance, two authors had the same idea for a plot of a novel, the law would protect how each had written the story, but not the plot itself.

Copyright exists from the moment a work is made and generally continues in existence until 50 years after the work's first publication or the author's death, whichever is the longer.

In the case of broadcasting, copyright remains in force for 70 years from the end of the calendar year in which the author died. Once the author has been dead for 70 years, all the works by that author go into the public domain, copyright no longer applies and no royalties need to be paid. Copyright is held indefinitely in an unpublished work. Note that copyright in some works is held by more than one person (the lyricist and the composer hold copyright in most songs). In such cases copyright remains in force for 70 years from the death of the longest surviving copyright holder.

There can be no copyright on news, so that even if we broadcast the story first, we cannot claim exclusivity of the facts, only the formulation of the words we used to tell the story. But if another station continually lifts the facts of all the stories we run without making any effort to compile the information for themselves, that might constitute an infringement of copyright.

The law allows us to use extracts from other people's works for the purpose of artistic criticism and review, or for covering news or current events. This falls within the category of fair dealing. In deciding how much of the work can be used 'fairly' before there is a breach of copyright, the courts look at the quality of what is used rather than the quantity. If in the course of a review only a small portion of the original work is used, but that portion is the vital part, that could be a breach of copyright. The law itself does not give any set figures as to what constitutes fair dealing, but the Society of Authors and the Publishers Association have agreed some practice guidelines. Quotations may be used so long as they do not add up to more than 400 words in total, or extracts of up to 800 words (so long as no individual extract is more than 300 words), would normally be acceptable. So would reading out fewer than 20 lines of a poem, so long as that was less than 25 per cent of the whole.

In 1991 the BBC tried to sue BSkyB for using very short extracts of BBC coverage of the World Cup Finals in news programmes. BSkyB credited the BBC and the extracts lasted between 14 and 37 seconds. The BBC was upset because it had paid nearly a million pounds for the broadcast rights, but the High Court Judge decided that BSkyB's use of short World Cup clips was fair dealing for the purpose of reporting current events. A 1994 case involving Time Warner Entertainment against Channel 4 television further extended the scope of fair dealing in a programme about Stanley Kubrick's *A Clockwork Orange*. Forty per cent of the programme included 6 per cent of the film and the High Court decided that serious criticism warranted this length of clips.

All broadcast stations should ask interviewees to sign 'contributors' consent forms' which give the radio station written consent for the material to be used for all broadcast and editing purposes.

In terms of news or current events, it has been held that copyright does not cover the information in a report, but rather the 'literary form in which the information is dressed'. In the compilation of reports, we can quote from documents so long as those documents have been circulated to a wide enough group to make them subject to public criticism. Do not forget that most government documents are HMSO copyright, even though government departments generally encourage wide coverage of their contents.

There have been cases in which even a document marked 'confidential', by being circulated to a progressively wider group of people has been deemed by the courts to have become well enough known to be open to public criticism. But, as in many other areas of law, each case will be decided on its own merits, so do not take foolhardy decisions on your own.

If the material in question is a commercially published disc or tape, whether it is the Spice Girls or Luciano Pavarotti, we have to record the title, author, publisher, disc or tape number, and the duration of what was played on air. It is on the basis of this information that the two main societies of copyright owners assess and collect royalties in order to redistribute the money among those who own the copyright. The societies are the Performing Right Society (PRS) and Phonographic Performance Ltd (PPL), and they also determine each station's 'needle time' (what proportion of air time can be given over to playing records), and how much the royalties should cost for that needle time.

Glossary

Radio is full of jargon or 'in' words. These are usually defined the first time they appear in the text, but you may need to refer back to this list from time to time.

actuality	Live or recorded sound of an event or speech as it happened.
ad	Advertisement.
ad lib	Unscripted remarks.
air check	A mention of a person, event or product on air.
ALC	Automatic level control. A feature on some portable tape machines that will automatically maintain a standard recording level.
alignment	The process of positioning tape heads or equipment controls for optimum performance.
AM	Amplitude Modulation. A method of radio transmission used on the Medium Wave system.
ambience	The low level background noise which characterises the sound in a room, studio or outside location.
Atmosphere or 'atmos'	Background noise or acoustic, usually used to recreate impression of a location to add immediacy/authenticity to a recording.
audio	Material transmitted or received as sound rather than the written word.
audio feed	Transmission of sound to other stations or studios.
back-anno or B/A	Announcement given at the end of a piece of music, a tape or interview which gives details of what has been heard.
back timing	The time at which an item (music or jingle)

	needs to be started (before it is needed or transmitted) so that it ends at a precise time (also known as prefading to time).
balance	(a) A mix of different sounds. (b) Desk control for altering the relative volume of left and right stereo channels.
band	(a) A separate section of tape within a spool; one of a number of separate items consecutively on the same tape. (b) Group of frequencies for transmission – wave band.
bass	Low frequency (LF) sound waves.
Basys	A popular newsroom computer system now being replaced by ENPS (Electronic News Production System).
bed	A theme or signature tune behind an announcer's voice that may be back-timed.
Billboard	(a) An American radio/record industry weekly magazine. (b) An IRN service of programme length material, fed to network stations each hour during weekdays.
booth	A small recording studio, usually designed to accommodate one or two people, for pre-recordings.
breaking story	A story that is happening now.
break-up	An audio fault causing sound to come and go intermittently.
bulk eraser	A machine designed to erase or 'wipe' a cassette, tape or cartridge all at once. Use with caution!
cans	Headphones.
capstan	Drive spindle on a tape machine.
cartridge	(a) A fixed duration, endless loop of tape on a spool in a sealed plastic case, available in different lengths, e.g. 40 secs or 100 secs. Nearly always referred to in abbreviated form as cart. (b) The head of a turntable arm which contains the stylus.
cassette	Reels of tape for a cassette recorder in a sealed plastic case.
catchline	Also known as slug. The word or words at the top of a script which identifies the story.
CD	Compact disc.
CD-ROM	Compact disc that you can only read from and not record on. Mostly used for information and data bases.

Glossary

Ceefax	BBC TV news and information text service receivable on teletext TVs.
Cellnet	A cellular telephone network which uses battery-operated telephones.
centre	(a) An adaptor for tape machines to enable them to take 10.5 inch spools, known as NAB spools. Hence also NAB centre or NAB adaptor. (b) An adaptor for 45 rpm discs with large centre hole.
channel	A single source on an audio desk.
clean feed	Output as it comes from the source or studio, without over-riding commentary or other incoming sources. Abbreviated to C/F.
clip	An extract from a programme or film.
copy	Written news or information.
cps	Centimetres per second. The speed at which tape is travelling past the heads, usually 19 cps for speech, and 38 cps for music (see ips).
cross-fade	Fading out one source while fading in a new one.
crosstalk	Interference caused by breakthrough of signals from one circuit or tape track to another.
cue	(a) Written introduction to a tape or live interview. (b) A signal by hand or by a light for the next item or person to begin.
cue programme	Programme or audio usually fed to a person's headphones that introduces or indicates when that person should start broadcasting, e.g. from a studio to an outside broadcast unit.
cut	A short excerpt from a longer item.
DAB	Digital Audio Broadcasting. Broadcasting by the digital encoding and decoding of signals.
DAT	Digital audio tape. Recording or reproducing with small cassette in the digital mode.
dB	Decibel. Unit of intensity of sound. Used to measure 'loudness'.
delay	Transmitting a programme three to ten seconds later than it happens live in order to be able to over-ride libels, profanities, etc. Also known as 'dump' or 'being in prof.'.
desk	An electronic control panel (and the furniture around it) for mixing different sources.

160 A Guide to Commercial Radio Journalism

	Also known as a mixer, panel or board.
distribution network	A network of audio circuits by which IRN can send out good quality audio material to all the ILR stations.
DJ	Disc jockey, sometimes called a jock.
double-header	Item or programme presented by two people.
drive time	Usually afternoon commuting time with the highest number of in-car listeners.
drop-out	A momentary break in the audio output of a tape caused by a fault or a bad splice.
dub	A copy from one source to another, i.e. cassette to disc, cassette to tape, tape to tape.
dur	Duration.
edit	To remove unwanted recorded material by digital means or by splicing the tape.
embargo	A request to hold publication of a fact or event until a specified date and time.
ENPS	Electronic News Production System. A computerised newsroom system for managing incoming stories, moving audio and editing text.
EQ	Equalisation. Using special controls to alter the sound quality, by increasing or decreasing sounds in the high, middle or low frequency sound ranges. Equivalent to the 'bass' and 'treble' controls on a domestic hi-fi.
erase	To remove all sound from a tape – on purpose or accidentally! Also known as wiping.
fader	Slide mechanism on the desk to alter the volume.
featurette	See wrap.
feed	Supply of audio by circuit or line.
feed-back	Same as 'howl-round'.
fixed spot	An item that regularly features in a programme.
fluff	To make a mistake while reading copy.
flutter	Accelerated version of wow.
FM	Frequency Modulation. A method of transmission used on VHF radio and some TV sound transmission.
full track	Recording which uses the full width of the tape.
FX	Sound effects, either intrinsic in the record-

	ing, or added from another source.
gram	Record turntable.
half-track	Method of recording which uses only half the width of the tape in one direction and the other half in the other direction, e.g. on cassette, but this is also a feature on some reel-to-reel machines.
hard disk	Computer disk for permanent storage of material.
hash	Crackling sound interference, like frying bacon.
head out or IVO	A tape which is rewound, ready to be played on a tape machine.
heads	(a) Parts of a tape recorder which erase, record and playback. (b) Headlines. One-sentence summaries of the main four or five stories. Also known as 'highlights'.
HF	(a) High frequency, the treble sounds. (b) The 'Short Wave' broadcasting band.
high level switcher	A switcher on a mixing desk enabling different or short-term external sources to be faded up on the desk, usually plugged through to the desk from MCR.
hiss	Background noise, usually barely discernible. Also known as 'tape hiss'.
howl-round	High-pitched tone created by high-level sounds feeding back through a live microphone.
hum	Low frequency tape interference, usually caused by electrical mains.
ID	Station identification.
ILR	Independent Local Radio.
in or in cue	The first few words of a tape or beginning of a record.
insert	A short live or recorded item in a programme, usually longer than a cut.
I/P	Input, where a signal enters a piece of equipment.
ips	Inches per second. The speed at which tape is travelling past the heads, usually 7½ ips for speech, and 15 ips for music (see cps).
IRN	Independent Radio News. The organisation which supplies national and international news to the ILR network.
ISDN	Integrated Services Digital Network. A system for providing high quality

	digital audio signals through telephone lines.
jack plug	A connecting plug used to route or re-route sources and/or destinations. A 'mini-jack' is normally used on cassette machines.
jingle	Short musical piece used to identify the programme, station or, in advertising, the product.
key	A switch.
kilo	A thousand, as in kilohertz, the frequency in thousands of cycles per second.
lead	(a) The first, and most important, story in a bulletin or programme. (b) An electrical cable from one piece of equipment to another, e.g. a 'microphone lead', 'supply lead', etc.
leader or leader tape	Tape of the same width as recording tape which indicates the beginning of an item (usually green), the end of an item (usually red), or bands within an item (usually yellow).
LED	Light emitting diode. A meter consisting of lines of lights indicating loudness.
legals	(a) The potential dangers of running foul of legal constraints in libel, contempt, etc. (b) Checking a tape for those dangers.
level	(a) The measurement of volume being recorded. (b) A prerecording check on a speaker's voice level, also known as 'level check' or 'taking some level'.
LF	(a) Low frequency, the bass sounds. (b) Long Wave transmissions.
link	A cue between items, usually items on a similar subject.
live	Happening now, i.e. not recorded.
log sheet	The sequence of ads which are decided by 'traffic'.
magnetic tape	Recording tape.
MCPS	Mechanical Copyright Protection Society. Licenses the reproduction of recorded sound.
MCR	Master Control Room. Where station output is usually monitored before being fed to the transmitter and where all outside sources are fed into and out again.
menu	Short tasters to indicate items to be

Glossary

	covered in a programme.
MF	Medium frequency, or the Medium Wave transmitting band.
mike rattle	Noise on a recording due to the misuse of the microphone.
Minidisc recorder	Portable machine which records on half size compact dics.
mix	The merging and balancing of two or more sounds or sources.
mixer	A piece of equipment with several sound channels which enables different sounds to be mixed.
modem	A device which can be connected to a computer to allow it to communicate with another computer on a telephone line (modulator/demodulator).
mono	Single line sound source, as opposed to stereo.
music log	Details of music broadcast for calculation of PPL rates, PRS and needletime.
needletime	The allocated time for the use of commercial discs.
news agency	An organisation that compiles and distributes news stories, locally, nationally or internationally.
OB	Outside broadcast.
off air	(a) Programme material heard or recorded from the radio. (b) General description for not being on-air, e.g. the off-air studio.
off mike	A speaker or noise either deliberately or accidentally not feeding directly into the microphone.
O/P	Output, where a signal emerges from a piece of equipment.
open reel	A tape recorder with two reels or spools, a supply (or feeder) spool and a take-up spool. Used to differentiate from cassette and cartridge machines. Also called reel-to-reel.
out	The last three words on a tape written as a warning that it is about to end.
out-times	The calculations in minutes and seconds for live speech to end so that the next item starts exactly on time, e.g. the on-hour news.
package	See wrap.
PA feed	A feed from the public address system at a

	conference where speakers will be using microphones running through it. Often requires special leads which need to be organised in advance.
para or par	Paragraph. As in 'Give me three short pars on that story'.
Parly	Parliament or IRN's Parliamentary unit; also extends to material from them, i.e. Parly wrap.
P as B	Programme as broadcast. A written record of all the items broadcast on a particular programme. Also known as the log.
patch cord	A lead with jack plugs at each end.
patching	Using patch cords to re-direct sound sources on a jack field or patch panel.
phone-op	The person in charge of the switchboard, usually used for on-air phone-ins.
plug	Free advertisement, also known as a puff.
popping	The sound of a sudden explosion of breath that results from being too close to the microphone, caused especially by words beginning with 'P' and 'B'.
pop-shield	See windshield.
pot	(a) End the transmission of a tape before the red leader. (b) Potentiometer: the volume control on a mixing desk channel.
PPL	Phonographic Performance Ltd. The organisation that licenses the broadcasting of sound recordings.
PPM	Peak Programme Meter. Indicates the loudness of audio material before it is transmitted.
PR	Public relations, or someone dealing with them (also PRO, Public Relations Office/Officer).
pre fade	The facility on mixing desks which allows a source to be heard before being faded up for transmission.
presser	A news conference.
prof.	See delay. Also short for 'prof. button', which initiates prof.
promo	Promotional. See trail.
prospects	A list of the day's stories to be covered.
PRS	Performing Rights Society. The organisation that collects royalties and redistributes the money to composers, publishers, per-

Glossary

	formers, etc.
Q & A	Question and answer; an interview.
quarter track	Method of recording which splits the tape into four bands. Not usually used in professional recordings.
RA	The Radio Authority.
Radio van or car	An OB vehicle capable of transmitting from the scene of a story to the studios.
RAJAR	Radio Audience Joint Research – the method of calculating audience size.
reel	The spool onto which tape is wound, usually 5, 7, or 10.5 inches. The smaller sizes are referred to as cine spools, the 10.5 inch is called a NAB spool.
reel-to-reel	See open reel.
ROT	Recorded Off Transmission, also known as 'off-air check'.
rumble	A low frequency vibration caused by the turntable motor.
running order	A record of the order of items to be broadcast on a programme, and each of their durations.
running story	A developing story that keeps changing which needs constant revision and updates.
script	The written text for a broadcast.
seg or segue	To go from one piece of audio and/or music straight to another without linking script.
slug	See catchline.
snap	A newsflash.
SOC	Standard Out Cue; e.g. 'Joe Bloggs, IRN, Madagascar'.
soundbite	A short piece of actuality, often 20 seconds or less, cut from an interview. See cut.
source	(a) A supplier of news information or ideas. (b) The origin of audio material.
splash	Sound caused by over-sibilance, usually with words beginning 'S' or 'C', or equipment fault.
splice	The cutting and re-joining of tape. Hence 'splicing block' and 'splicing tape'.
spool	See reel.
sportsbox	Small portable mixer connected to an ISDN line, often used for coverage at sports grounds.
spot	(a) An advertisement. (b) An item regularly

	appearing in a programme, also known as 'fixed spot'.
stab	A short ID or jingle.
sting	A short sequence of musical chords.
stringer	A freelance covering an area where there is no staff reporter available.
tail-ender	A light piece of news at the end of a programme or bulletin.
tail out or T/O	A tape that needs to be rewound before it can be played because it is on the reel backwards.
talk back	A communication system, either between control room and studio, or between adjacent studios, offices, etc.
TBU	Telephone Balancing Unit. Device to enable better quality two-way telephone reports or interviews.
tease or teaser	Short headline or highlight at top of a programme to grab listeners' attention.
Teletext	ITV's on-screen text based information service.
tone	A signal used to synchronise levels between two sources.
top and tail	To attach leader tape against the first sound required on a recorded tape, to edit the tape, and then attach leader tape against the last sound required.
tops	The higher frequency sounds of speech.
traffic	(a) The department that decides placement of ads on a log sheet according to each client's contract. (b) Reports on road traffic.
trail	A promotional 'spot' for a forthcoming programme. Also known as a 'promo'.
treble	High frequency sound waves.
TX	Transmission or transmitter.
UHF	Ultra High Frequency radio band.
update	A revised report with new information on a running story.
VHF	Very High Frequency band.
voicebank	System used by emergency services to provide information on incidents.
voicer	A report using scripted copy read by a reporter or presenter without actuality.
vox pops	'Voice of the people'. Reactions of people on the street edited together to provide a montage of opinions on a topic. Vox pops

	should not be presented as a representative sample.
VU	Volume Unit meter. Measures the average loudness of sound.
waveform	Visual display of recorded sound on computer editing program.
wavelength	The metered band used for tuning to a particular frequency.
wild track	Recording of the atmosphere on a location to be used as background noise later on.
windshield	A microphone cover, usually foam rubber, to protect against wind noise.
wipe	See erase.
wire services	National or international news gathering organisations which send stories by either teleprinter or computer.
wow	A recording fault which results in speed variations.
wrap	A report that includes more than one piece of actuality, linked by the reporter. Also known as a package or featurette.

Further reading

Andrew Boyd, *Broadcast Journalism – Techniques of Radio and TV News*, Focal Press, 1997
Peter Carey, *Media Law*, Sweet and Maxwell, 1996
Paul Chantler and Sim Harris, *Local Radio Journalism*, Focal Press, 1996
Andrew Crissell, *Understanding Radio*, Routledge, 1994
Tim Crook, *International Radio Journalism*, Routledge, 1998
Sir Ernest Gowers, *The Complete Plain Words*, Pelican Books. Originally an attempt to get Civil Servants to use ordinary but proper language. It is better not to dip into this book unless you have some time to enjoy the clever barbs it employs in pointing out the misuse of everyday English
Walter Greenwood and Tom Welsh, *McNae's Essential Law for Journalists*, 14th edition, Butterworths, 1995. This is widely regarded as the journalist's 'bible' on the law. It is compact and understandable to those of us not legally trained. Remember, though, that it is aimed at print journalists, so the section on election law, for example, does not apply to radio. Although this edition was published at a time when the law was in the midst of many changes, their reading of the eventual outcome is correct
The Guardian Media Guide, Fourth Estate (published annually)
John Hartley, *Understanding News*, Routledge, 1995
Wynford Hicks, *English for Journalists*, Routledge, 1998
John Kingdom, *Government and Politics in Britain*, Polity Press, 1991
Robert McLeish, *The Technique of Radio Production*, 3rd edition, Focal Press, 1993
David Northmore, *Lifting the Lid: a guide to investigative research*, Cassell, 1996
Geoffrey Robertson and Andrew Nicol, *Media Law*, 3rd edition, Penguin, 1992
Keith Waterhouse, *Waterhouse on Newspaper Style*, Viking, 1986. This guide for tabloid papers is largely applicable to writing for any medium
John Wilson, *Understanding Journalism*, Routledge, 1996

Index

20:20:20 minute format, xiii, 69

Abbreviations, 21–2
Abstractions in scripts, 19
Accord and satisfaction, as libel defence, 126
Accuracy in reporting, 46–7, 52, 83, 84, 85, 88, 121–2
Actuality, 31, 47, 49, 55
Administration of Justice Act, 1925, 113
Advertisements, 5, 62–3, 71, 73, 87
Advertising revenue, xv
Advice items, 76, 80
AKG D230, 4
AltaVista, 36, 41
American commercial radio, xiii, xv
Analogies in scripts, 19
Angle of the story, 44, 49, 61
Anonymity, see Identifying people
Apologies, 92, 126, 127
Archiving, 7, 24, 43
Artistic criticism, 155
Associated Press, 30
Associations, reference sources, 42
Atmospherics, 56
Audio distribution, 2
Audio service, 30
Audio Technica, 4
Audiovault, 13
Australian commercial radio, xiii, xv

Back-announcing, 74
Balance, 56, 141
  BSC code on, 89

time allocations, 142–3, 144, 145, 146
wraps, balanced, 143, 146
Bar Council, 100
Barristers, 100, 111
Battery life, 4
BBC, xiii
  copyright, 154, 155
  Producers' Guidelines, 88
Behaviour, see Journalists, conduct
Bill of Rights, 1688, 124
Bimedia arrangements, xiv, 31
Brand names, 81
British Telecom, 15
Broadcast Standards Commission, 93
Broadcast Standards Council, 93
Broadcasting Acts (1981, 1990), 141, 146
Broadcasting Standards Commission (BSC), Code on Fairness and Privacy, 88–90
  complaints and inquiries, 93
Bulk erasers, 9
Bulletins, see News, bulletins

Cans, see Headphones
Capital Radio, xiii
Cartridge players, 5
Carts, 5, 6, 56–7, 67
Cassette tape, 3–4
CD players, 5
CD-ROM reference sources, 41
Ceefax, 28
Check calls, 47
Check-lists, 66

Chequebook journalism, 91
Children, 149
  identifying in reports, 150, 151–2
Children Act, 1989, 151
Children and Young Persons Acts (1933, 1969), 147, 150
City news, *see* Financial coverage
Civil courts, 95, 98–9
  contempt of, 134, 137
  court procedure, 102
  proceedings being active in, 135, 137
Civil law, 95, 98–9
Classic FM, sample of running order, 63, 64
Cliches, 17
CNN, 31
Commentaries, 71
Commercial radio, compared to BBC, 27
Committal proceedings, 96–7
  reporting to avoid contempt, 132–3
  Scotland, 109
Common Law contempt, 138–9
  imminence, 139
Communication, 10, *see also* Talk-back
Community involvement, 27, 50
Complaints, 88, 92–3
Computer impacts, 1, 5, 12–13
Confidentiality, 85–6
Contacts, 27, 44–5, 50
  in court reporting, 110–12, 147
  revealing sources, 85–6
Contempt of court, 15–16, 80, 115, 131–40
  common law, 138–9
  defences to, 137–8
Contempt of Court Act, 1981, 85, 113, 114, 131–2, 134–5, 136, 140, 147, 148
Control rooms, 5, 6
Convention on Human Rights, 107
CoolEditPro, 13
Copyright, 46, 154–6
Copyright Act 1988, 154–5
Coroner's Inquests, 105–6
  contempt of, 152
  proceedings being active in, 152
Corrections, publication of, 126
County courts, 98, 100, 151
Court of Appeal, 97–8, 99, 129

  contempt of, 137
Court of Criminal Appeal, Scotland, 108
Court reporting, conduct in, 112–13, 114, 115
Court Reporting Agency, 111
Crime reporting:
  court staff, 110–12, 147
  criminals, 91–2
  police, 111, 126
  witnesses, 91
Crime (Sentences) Act, 1997, 150
Crimes against property, definitions, 103
Crimes against the person, definitions, 102–3
Criminal courts, 95–8
  contempt of, 131–6
  court procedure, 101–2
  proceedings being active in, 134–5, 137
Criminal Justice Act:
  1987, 150
  1988, 148
  1991, 151
Criminal Justice and Public Order Act, 1994, 148
Criminal law, 95
Criminal Procedures and Investigations Act, 1996, 151, 152
Cross-media ownership, xv
Crown court, 96–7, 100, 148
  appeals from juvenile court, 150
  contempt of, 133–4
  preliminary and pre-trial hearings, 150–1
  records and notices of orders, 147
Crown Prosecution Service (CPS), 100, 112
Cues, 5, 22–4, 63, 67, 72, 73–4
Current affairs, xiii

DAB, xiv
Dalet computerised newsroom systems, 13, 14
Damages, 128–9
DAT recorders, *see* Sony DAT recorders
DAVE audio editing system, 13, 70
Dcarts, 6

Decision making, 15
Defamation Act, 1952, 116, 117, 121, 126, 127, 129
Defamation Act, 1996, 116, 117, 124, 125, 126, 128, 129
DejaNews, 41
Delayed broadcast, 15–16
Diaries, see News diaries
Diaxys, 12
Digital Broadcasting, see DAB
Digital recordings, 3
Digital editing, 12–13, 14
Digital equipment, 2, 5, 6, 15–16
Directories, 41–3
Disability Discrimination Act, 1995, 152
Disasters, 50–1, 73, 84, 86–7
    public inquiries, 105
Discussion of public affairs, as contempt defence, 137
Discussion programmes, xiii, 71, 89
District courts, Scotland, 107–8
Divorce proceedings, reporting restrictions, 151
Documentaries, 71
Domestic news, 27, see also Local news; National news
Domestic proceedings, 151–2
Door-stepping, 48
Double sourcing material, 46, 83
Drama, 71
Dubbing, 11–12

E-mail, 28
Editing, 12–14, 56
    digital, 12–13
    software programmes, 13
    tape, 14
Editors, xiv, 29, 31, 44, 52, 55, 58, 59, 142
Election campaigns, reporting, 141–6
Election candidates, 144–5
Election logs, 143, 145–6
Electronic personal organisers, 44–5
Embargoes, 12, 45–6
Emergency services, 47, 48
    radio frequencies, 90
Engineers, 10, 15, 23, 63, 66, 67
    relationship with journalists, 2
Entertainment items, xiii, xiv, 30
    reference sources, 42–3

Equal time allocations, 142, 144, see also Balance, time allocations
Erasing, 6, 8
European Convention of Human Rights, xv
European Court of Human Rights, 86, 107, 128–9
European Court of Justice, 106
European law, 106, 107
Excite (search engine), 41

Faders, 9–10
Fair comment, as libel defence, 122–3
Family law cases, 151
Fatal Accident Enquiries (Scotland), 152
Faxes, 28
Features, 29, 71
Financial coverage, xiii, 29, 30
Foreign news, 21, 27, 30, 31, 58, 59
    reference sources, 42
Format, 60, 61, 63, 69–71, 73, 74, 79
Fraud cases, 150–1
Freedom of Information Bill, 153–4
Freelance journalists:
    copyright and, 154
    tip-offs from, 47

Gap-filling, 16
Government institutions, 46, 50
    freedom of information, 153–4
    libel, 126
    spokespersons, 144
Guests, see Interviewees

Hallam FM/Magic 1458 AM, Sheffield, 1, 9, 14
Headlines:
    first sentences as, 20
    IRN's supply of, 31
Headphones, 10, 70
High Court, 99, 120, 129, 135, 152, 156
    appeals from juvenile court, 150
    Family Division of, 151
High Court of Justiciary (Scotland), 107
HotBot (search engine), 41
Hot Keys, 63, 70

House of Lords, 98, 99
   contempt of, 137
Human Rights Act, 107

Identifiable sound of a station, 72
Identification passes, 113
Identifying people, 20, 52, 132
   anonymity, 147
   children and young persons, 150
   in child abuse cases, 152
   in disability discrimination cases, 152
   in domestic and family cases, 151
   in libel cases, 119
   in rape and other sex offence cases, 148–9
   labelling (racial, sexual, religious), 87
ILR stations, 7, 58, 154
Impartiality, 85, 141, *see also* Balance
Independent Broadcasting Authority, *see* IBA
Independent Media Distribution, 30
InfoSeek, 41
Initials, *see* Abbreviations
Innocent dissemination, as libel defence, 127–8
Inquiries, 103–5
   planning, 104–5
   proceedings active in, 135
   public, 105
Integrated Services Digital Network, *see* ISDN
International news, *see* Foreign news
Internet:
   as a resource, xv, 31–41, 42, 43
   distribution of IRN, xiv
   double sourcing material from, 46
   search engines, 33, 34, 35, 41
Interviewees, 50–1, 52, 54, 55, 76, 80
   at court, 113–14
   barristers, 100, 111
   consent, 90, 156
   judges, 110–11
   jurors, 140
   officials, 49, 50
   personalities, 51, 76
   politicians, 49, 76
   position in the studio, 6, 54
   pressure group representatives, 49
   protocol for dealing with, 88
   solicitors, 100, 111–12
Interviews, 12, 50–5
   advance list of questions, 49, 51
   at a distance, xiv
   boring, 6
   emotional, 50–1
   eye contact during, 10, 54, 56
   face-to-face, xiv, 9, 10–11
   live, 74
      and libel, 126–8
   phone-outs, 9, 30, 55–6
   pre-interview interviews, 74
   pre-recorded, 56
   questions, 12, 50–1, 53–4, 57
   RA guidelines for, 10, 51
   styles, 71–2
IRN, xiv, 28, 31, 58, 146
   distribution, xiv, 2
   news cut length, 55, 58
   prospects list, 28
   web site, 32, 39
   wrap length, 58
ISDN circuits, 2, 113
ITN, xiv, 31

Jingles, 5, 16
Job distinctions, xiv, 68–9
Journalists, 29, 55
   civil rights, 82, 94
   conduct, 48, 50–1, 54, 82–93, 112–13, 114, 115
   copyright, 154
   craft of, 44–59
   freelance, 47, 154
   nerves, 54
   numbers of, xiv
   objectivity, 53, 83, 84–5
   opinions of, 50, 53, 83–4
   role, xiv, xv, 68–9
   salaries, xiv
   self-op booth, 7, 9–10
Judges:
   circuit, 97, 99
   County Courts, 98
   Court of Appeal, 98
   criticism of, 139
   High Court, 97, 99, 129
   House of Lords, 98
   solicitors becoming, 101

titles, 99
Juries, 96, 97, 136, 152
  awarding damages, 128–9
  Coroner's Court, 105, 152
  County Courts, 98, 102
  Crown Courts, 97, 101–2
  Scotland, 108
Justification, as libel defence, 121–2
Juvenile Courts, 149–50

Landline distribution of IRN, xiv
Language, 12, 17, 19, 21, 24, 74, 82, 132
  abbreviations, 21–2
  colloquial, 27
  contractions, 18
  in interviews, 50–1, 53, 54, 57
  legal terminology, 94
  libel, 15–16, 118, 132
  swearing, 15–16, 81, 91
Law Society, 100
Law Society of Scotland, 94
Leader tape, 8
Leads and plugs, 11
Legal aid, 95, 104, 129
Legal definitions, 94, 102–3
  differences between Scotland and England/Wales, 107, 108, 130
Libel, xv, 15–16, 80, 116–30
  damages for, 128–9
  defences to 120–8
  definition of, 117
  liability for in radio broadcasting, 117, 119
  proof of, 119
Libel Amendment Act, 1888, 124
Links, 55, 72, 73, 74
Listeners, 60
  addressing an individual, 18, 73
  complaints, 88, 92–3
  choice of, 83
  early morning, 71
  involvement, 72–3, 82
  national and local, 58, 59
  sensibilities, 73, 84, 87
  tip-offs from, 47
  trust, 83
  young people, 90–1
Live broadcasting, xiv, 53, 74, 129
Local knowledge, see Community involvement
Local news, 58, see also Domestic news; National news
Local radio stations network, xiv, 58
Logging tapes, 7
Logical progression, 18, 53, 74, see also Order of material

Magazine programmes, 71–2, 73–5
Magistrates, 96, 99
Magistrates Courts, 95–7, 100, 132–3
  domestic proceedings, 151
  fraud cases, 150
  records and notices of orders, 147
Magistrates Courts Act, 1980, 97, 132–4
Malice, 125
Malicious falsehood, 129
Management, 27, 90, 142, 145
Managing editors, xiv
Marantz cassette recorders, 3, 4
Media law, 112
Medical treatment, reporting, 91
Members of Parliament, see Politicians
Meters, 4–5
  peak programme meters (PPMs), 5
  volume units (VUs), 5
Metro and Bloomberg, 30
Microphones, 4, 6, 66, 70
  hidden, 90
  positioning, 48, 54
Minidisc players, 5
Minidisc recorders, see Sony Minidisc recorders
Mixing desks, 5, 6
Mixture of items, 58, 59, 74, 75
Motoring offences, 103
Music, 56, 62,
  copyright, 68, 156
  needle time, 156
  reference sources, 43
  see also Jingles

Naming people, see Identifying people
National news, 31, 58, 59, see also Domestic news; Local news
Needle time, 156
Network stations, 28, 31
Networked systems, 2

News, 28, 55, 58–9, 82–3, 88, 144–5, 146
  bulletins, xiii, 31, 58
  no copyright of, 155, 156
  twenty-four hour format, xiii
News conferences, 46, 48–9
News cuts, 55
News diaries, 27–8
News releases, 27–8, 45–6
News wires, 28–31, 46–7
Newsdesks, 29, 58
NewsDirect 97.3, 69, 70
Newspapers, 29, 48
  cuttings libraries, 43
  web sites, 33, 40
Newsrooms, 1, 9–10, 29, 70
  news production booths, 6–7
Noises, unwanted, 10–11, 56
Northern Ireland and terrorism reporting, 84, 153
Notebooks, 114–15
Numbers in scripts, 18, 20, 25, 83

Official Secrets Act, 1989, 86, 153
Officials, protection of, 147–8
Open-reel tape machines, 5, 6, 7, 8
Order of material, 12, 57, see also Running order
Out-times, 62, 63
Overseas legal proceedings, reporting, 125–6

Pace, 27, 72–3, 76, 79
Parliamentary coverage, 31, see also Election campaigns, reporting
Pending period for elections, 141–2
People:
  reference sources, 41
  see also Contacts; Identifying people
Performing Rights Society, 156
Phone operators, 66, 79, 128
Phone-ins, xiii, 66, 67, 71, 75–81, 127–8, 129
  BSC directive on, 89
  election times, 143, 145–6
  guests, see Interviewees
  profanity button, 15–16, 77, 80–81
  retrospective comment, 75
Phone lines, quality, 77
Phone logs, 78–9

Phone-outs, 9, 30, 55–6
Phone votes, 76
Phonographic Performance Ltd, 156
Pleas of mitigation allegations, 152
Police and Criminal Evidence Act, 85, 156
Police as contacts, 111, 126
  Public Relations Bureau, 111
Politicians:
  advance lists of questions, 49
  election candidates, 144–5
  party spokespersons, 144
  privilege, 123, 124
  reference sources, 41
Portable equipment, 3–4
Pots, 22
Preliminary hearings, reporting restrictions, 150–1
Presentation, 55–9
  pace, 27, 72–3
  style, 18, 20–1, 58, 59, 61, 71–2
  timing, 22
  tone, 18, 24, 54
Presenters, 15, 23, 66, 67, 69, 70, 72, 73, 78, 79–80, 89
  position in the studio, 6
Press Association:
  news wire, 28, 29
  prospects list, 28
Press conferences, see News conferences
Press releases, see News releases
Pressure groups, 49
Pre-trial hearings, reporting restrictions, 150–1
Prevention of Terrorism (Temporary Provisions) Act, 1989, 152–3
Privacy, 90, 93
Privilege, as libel defence, 123–6
  absolute, 124–5
  qualified, 125–6
PRnet Newswire, 33, 37
Procurator-Fiscal, 108, 109, 112
Producers, 10, 15, 23, 29, 44, 56, 60–81, 128
Production booths, 6–7
Profanity button, 15–16, 77, 80
Programme as Broadcast (P as B), 68
Programme controllers, xiv, 78

Programme planning, 60, 61, 74–5
Prospects lists, 28
Public interest, 89
   as libel defence, 122–3, 153
Public service broadcasts, 28
Publications, reference sources, 41–3
Pulses, *see* Cues

Quantity of material, 31
Questions, *see* Interviews, questions
Quotations, 20
   reference sources, 43

Radio, compared to other media, 20, 49, 50, 82, 112, 141, 146
Radio Authority, 142
   complaints procedure, 92–3
   copyright, 154
   guidelines, 10, 15, 51, 62, 63, 78, 87, 90
Radio web sites, 32, 33, 39
Rape offences, 87, 148–9
RCS editing systems, 13
RealAudio News, 33
Reception, quality, xiv
Reconstructions, 85
Recorders, portable, 3–4
Recording at the scene, 48
   court proceedings, 113–14, 135
Reference sources, 41–3, 46
Rehabilitation of Offenders Act, 1974, 149
Remote stations, programming, xv
Repetition, 17, 19, 20, 24
Reporters, *see* Journalists
Reporting restrictions, 85, 97, 141–56
   and contempt, 133–4
   at election times, 141–6
   in juvenile courts, 150
   in preliminary and pre-trial hearings, 150–1
   in rape cases, 148–9
   orders, 147–8
Representation of the People Act (RPA), 1983, 141, 142, 144, 146
Research, 52, *see also* Reference sources
Reuters, 28, 30, 31

Reviews, 155
Revox PR99BV, 7, 8
Rolling news, xiii, 69
Royalties, 68, 154, 156
Running order, 31, 58, 59, 62–6, 73, *see also* Order of material
Running time, 23, 24, 58

Sadie ProTools, 12
Salaries, xiv
Satellite distribution of IRN, xiv, 2
Scandalising the courts, 139
Scene of the story, technique, 47–8
Scottish law, 94, 107–9
   contempt, 140
   libel, 129–30
Scripts, writing, 17–24, 58, *see also* Interviews, questions
Security services, 86, 153–4
Self-op booths, 7, 9–10
Sexual harassment cases, reporting, 152
Sexual offences, reporting, 87, 90, 93, 149, 150, 151
Sexual Offences (Amendment) Act, 1976, 148
Sexual Offences (Amendment) Act, 1992, 149
Sheriff Courts, Scotland, 107–8, 130
Showbusiness items, xiv, 51
   reference sources, 42–3
Silly seasons, 49–50
Simplicity in scripts, 18, 19–21, 53
Simulations, 85
Slugs, 63
Society of Authors and Publishers Association, 155
Solicitors, 100–1
   consulting, 126
Sony DAT (Digital Audio Tape) recorders, 3, 4, 10
   displays, 5
Sony Minidisc recorders, 3, 4, 10
   displays, 5
Sony Pro Walkman, 3, 4
Sound archives, 7, 24, 43
Sound effects, 56, 62
Sound levels, 4–5, 9, 10, 52, 66
Sound pictures, 18
Sound quality, 2–3, 4, 55, 56, 77
Sources, *see* Contacts; Reference sources
Speech rhythms, natural, 12

Splicing, 8, 14
Spokespersons, 125
Sponsorship, xv
Sports items, xiii, xiv, 29, 30
   numbers in, 25
Spycatcher case, 82, 86, 138-9
Stand-by items, 67
Statistics in scripts, 18, 20
Stings, 62, 63
Story selection, 31
Story-telling, 19-22, 44-59
   freshening, 58
   updating, 58
Studer A801s, 7
Studios, 5, 6
   discipline, 15, 67
   layout, 6
   operational skills, 69
   production, 66-70
Style, 18, 20-1, 58, 59, 61, 71-2
   conversational, 18
   distinctive sound, 72
Substantial risk, as contempt defence, 137-8
Surveillance and monitoring, 90, 153
Swearing, 15-16

Talk Radio, sample running order, 63, 65
Talk-back, 6, 66, 67
Tapes, magnetic, 1, 2, 3, 66
   leader tape, 8
   logging tapes, 7
   organisation of, 63, 67, 68
Telephone technique, 45-6
Teletext, 28
Television as a source, 28, 31
Television reports on radio, xiv
Tense, present, 20-1
Terrorism, 84, 152-3
Time limitations, 58, 59, 61, 78
Time of day, 71
Tone, 18, 54, 73
   conversational, 18, 24

Trade Union Reform and Employment Rights Act, 1993, 152
Trails, 5, 62
Training and education, xiv
Treasure trove, 106
Tribunals, 100, 103-4
   employment, 99
   industrial, 104, 152
   proceedings being active in, 135
Two-Ten Communications, 30

Understanding:
   interviewee's, 53
   listener's, 18, 19, 20,
   presenter's, 24
Unintentional libel, as libel defence, 126
Updating a story, 58

Video tape, 7
Violence, reporting, 87, 90, 93
Voices:
   intonation, 24, 74
   levels, 66
   of interviewees, 52
   pauses, 24
   popping, 25
   projection, 25
   reading a script, 24
   register, 25-6
   speed of delivery, 24-5
   see also Presentation
Vox pops, 57

Webcrawler, 33, 35
Wild-tracking, 56
Wireless Telegraphy Act, 1949, 90
Word usage, see Language
Work experience, xiv
Wraps, 55, 56-7, 74, 143
   balanced, 143, 146

Yahoo! UK & Ireland, 33, 34, 41
Young persons, 91, 149-50

For Product Safety Concerns and Information please contact our EU
representative GPSR@taylorandfrancis.com
Taylor & Francis Verlag GmbH, Kaufingerstraße 24, 80331 München, Germany

www.ingramcontent.com/pod-product-compliance
Lightning Source LLC
Chambersburg PA
CBHW061447300426
44114CB00014B/1877